Saddam Hussein

Charles J. Shields

CHELSEA HOUSE
PUBLISHERS
A Haights Cross Communications Company

Philadelphia

Frontispiece: Saddam Hussein has been president of Iraq since 1979. He refuses to let the United States bully him and envisions himself as the leader of the Arab world.

CHELSEA HOUSE PUBLISHERS

EDITOR IN CHIEF Sally Cheney
DIRECTOR OF PRODUCTION Kim Shinners
CREATIVE MANAGER Takeshi Takahashi
MANUFACTURING MANAGER Diann Grasse

Staff for SADDAM HUSSEIN

EDITOR Lee Marcott
ASSOCIATE EDITOR Bill Conn
PRODUCTION ASSISTANT Jaimie Winkler
PICTURE RESEARCH 21st Century Publishing and Communications, Inc.
SERIES DESIGNER Takeshi Takahashi
COVER DESIGNER Keith Trego
LAYOUT 21st Century Publishing and Communications, Inc.

A Haights Cross Communications 🕇 Company

http://www.chelseahouse.com

3 5 7 9 8 6 4 2

Library of Congress Cataloging-in-Publication Data

Shields, Charles J., 1951–
  Saddam Hussein / Charles J. Shields.
    p. cm.—(Major world leaders)
Summary: Describes the life of the leader of Iraq, from his childhood, through his rise to power, the Iran-Iraq War, the Persian Gulf War, to his ongoing presidency.
Includes bibliographical references and index.
  ISBN 0-7910-6943-5
  1. Hussein, Saddam, 1937–   —Juvenile literature. 2. Presidents—Iraq—Biography—Juvenile literature. [1. Hussein, Saddam, 1937–   2. Presidents—Iraq.] I. Title. II. Series.
DS79.66.H87 S58 2002
956.7044'092—dc21

2002008447

TABLE OF CONTENTS

On Leadership

Arthur M. Schlesinger, jr.

Leadership, it may be said, is really what makes the world go round. Love no doubt smoothes the passage; but love is a private transaction between consenting adults. Leadership is a public transaction with history. The idea of leadership affirms the capacity of individuals to move, inspire, and mobilize masses of people so that they act together in pursuit of an end. Sometimes leadership serves good purposes, sometimes bad; but whether the end is benign or evil, great leaders are those men and women who leave their personal stamp on history.

Now, the very concept of leadership implies the proposition that individuals can make a difference. This proposition has never been universally accepted. From classical times to the present day, eminent thinkers have regarded individuals as no more than the agents and pawns of larger forces, whether the gods and goddesses of the ancient world or, in the modern era, race, class, nation, the dialectic, the will of the people, the spirit of the times, history itself. Against such forces, the individual dwindles into insignificance.

So contends the thesis of historical determinism. Tolstoy's great novel *War and Peace* offers a famous statement of the case. Why, Tolstoy asked, did millions of men in the Napoleonic Wars, denying their human feelings and their common sense, move back and forth across Europe slaughtering their fellows? "The war," Tolstoy answered, "was bound to happen simply because it was bound to happen." All prior history determined it. As for leaders, they, Tolstoy said, "are but the labels that serve to give a name to an end and, like labels, they have the least possible connection with the event." The greater the leader, "the more conspicuous the inevitability and the predestination of every act he commits." The leader, said Tolstoy, is "the slave of history."

Determinism takes many forms. Marxism is the determinism of class. Nazism the determinism of race. But the idea of men and women as the slaves of history runs athwart the deepest human instincts. Rigid determinism abolishes the idea of human freedom—the assumption of free choice that underlies every move we make, every word we speak, every thought we think. It abolishes the idea of human responsibility,

since it is manifestly unfair to reward or punish people for actions that are by definition beyond their control. No one can live consistently by any deterministic creed. The Marxist states prove this themselves by their extreme susceptibility to the cult of leadership.

More than that, history refutes the idea that individuals make no difference. In December 1931 a British politician crossing Fifth Avenue in New York City between 76th and 77th Streets around 10:30 P.M. looked in the wrong direction and was knocked down by an automobile—a moment, he later recalled, of a man aghast, a world aglare: "I do not understand why I was not broken like an eggshell or squashed like a gooseberry." Fourteen months later an American politician, sitting in an open car in Miami, Florida, was fired on by an assassin; the man beside him was hit. Those who believe that individuals make no difference to history might well ponder whether the next two decades would have been the same had Mario Constasino's car killed Winston Churchill in 1931 and Giuseppe Zangara's bullet killed Franklin Roosevelt in 1933. Suppose, in addition, that Lenin had died of typhus in Siberia in 1895 and that Hitler had been killed on the western front in 1916. What would the 20th century have looked like now?

For better or for worse, individuals do make a difference. "The notion that a people can run itself and its affairs anonymously," wrote the philosopher William James, "is now well known to be the silliest of absurdities. Mankind does nothing save through initiatives on the part of inventors, great or small, and imitation by the rest of us—these are the sole factors in human progress. Individuals of genius show the way, and set the patterns, which common people then adopt and follow."

Leadership, James suggests, means leadership in thought as well as in action. In the long run, leaders in thought may well make the greater difference to the world. "The ideas of economists and political philosophers, both when they are right and when they are wrong," wrote John Maynard Keynes, "are more powerful than is commonly understood. Indeed the world is ruled by little else. Practical men, who believe themselves to be quite exempt from any intellectual influences, are usually the slaves of some defunct economist. . . . The power of vested interests is vastly exaggerated compared with the gradual encroachment of ideas."

But, as Woodrow Wilson once said, "Those only are leaders of men, in the general eye, who lead in action. . . . It is at their hands that new thought gets its translation into the crude language of deeds." Leaders in thought often invent in solitude and obscurity, leaving to later generations the tasks of imitation. Leaders in action—the leaders portrayed in this series—have to be effective in their own time.

And they cannot be effective by themselves. They must act in response to the rhythms of their age. Their genius must be adapted, in a phrase from William James, "to the receptivities of the moment." Leaders are useless without followers. "There goes the mob," said the French politician, hearing a clamor in the streets. "I am their leader. I must follow them." Great leaders turn the inchoate emotions of the mob to purposes of their own. They seize on the opportunities of their time, the hopes, fears, frustrations, crises, potentialities. They succeed when events have prepared the way for them, when the community is awaiting to be aroused, when they can provide the clarifying and organizing ideas. Leadership completes the circuit between the individual and the mass and thereby alters history.

It may alter history for better or for worse. Leaders have been responsible for the most extravagant follies and most monstrous crimes that have beset suffering humanity. They have also been vital in such gains as humanity has made in individual freedom, religious and racial tolerance, social justice, and respect for human rights.

There is no sure way to tell in advance who is going to lead for good and who for evil. But a glance at the gallery of men and women in MAJOR WORLD LEADERS suggests some useful tests.

One test is this: Do leaders lead by force or by persuasion? By command or by consent? Through most of history leadership was exercised by the divine right of authority. The duty of followers was to defer and to obey. "Theirs not to reason why/Theirs but to do and die." On occasion, as with the so-called enlightened despots of the 18th century in Europe, absolutist leadership was animated by humane purposes. More often, absolutism nourished the passion for domination, land, gold, and conquest and resulted in tyranny.

The great revolution of modern times has been the revolution of equality. "Perhaps no form of government," wrote the British historian James Bryce in his study of the United States, *The American Commonwealth*, "needs great leaders so much as democracy." The idea that all people should be equal in their legal condition has undermined the old structure of authority, hierarchy, and deference. The revolution of equality has had two contrary effects on the nature of leadership. For equality, as Alexis de Tocqueville pointed out in his great study *Democracy in America*, might mean equality in servitude as well as equality in freedom.

"I know of only two methods of establishing equality in the political world," Tocqueville wrote. "Rights must be given to every citizen, or none at all to anyone . . . save one, who is the master of all." There was no middle ground "between the sovereignty of all and the absolute power of one man." In his astonishing prediction of 20th-century totalitarian dictatorship, Tocqueville explained how the revolution of equality could lead to the *Führerprinzip* and more terrible absolutism than the world had ever known.

But when rights are given to every citizen and the sovereignty of all is established, the problem of leadership takes a new form, becomes more exacting than ever before. It is easy to issue commands and enforce them by the rope and the stake, the concentration camp and the *gulag*. It is much harder to use argument and achievement to overcome opposition and win consent. The Founding Fathers of the United States understood the difficulty. They believed that history had given them the opportunity to decide, as Alexander Hamilton wrote in the first Federalist Paper, whether men are indeed capable of basing government on "reflection and choice, or whether they are forever destined to depend . . . on accident and force."

Government by reflection and choice called for a new style of leadership and a new quality of followership. It required leaders to be responsive to popular concerns, and it required followers to be active and informed participants in the process. Democracy does not eliminate emotion from politics; sometimes it fosters demagoguery; but it is confident that, as the greatest of democratic leaders put it, you cannot fool all of the people all of the time. It measures leadership by results and retires those who overreach or falter or fail.

It is true that in the long run despots are measured by results too. But they can postpone the day of judgment, sometimes indefinitely, and in the meantime they can do infinite harm. It is also true that democracy is no guarantee of virtue and intelligence in government, for the voice of the people is not necessarily the voice of God. But democracy, by assuring the right of opposition, offers built-in resistance to the evils inherent in absolutism. As the theologian Reinhold Niebuhr summed it up, "Man's capacity for justice makes democracy possible, but man's inclination to justice makes democracy necessary."

A second test for leadership is the end for which power is sought. When leaders have as their goal the supremacy of a master race or the promotion of totalitarian revolution or the acquisition and exploitation of colonies or the protection of greed and privilege or the preservation of personal power, it is likely that their leadership will do little to advance the cause of humanity. When their goal is the abolition of slavery, the liberation of women, the enlargement of opportunity for the poor and powerless, the extension of equal rights to racial minorities, the defense of the freedoms of expression and opposition, it is likely that their leadership will increase the sum of human liberty and welfare.

Leaders have done great harm to the world. They have also conferred great benefits. You will find both sorts in this series. Even "good" leaders must be regarded with a certain wariness. Leaders are not demigods; they put on their trousers one leg after another just like ordinary mortals. No leader is infallible, and every leader needs to be reminded of this at regular intervals. Irreverence irritates leaders but is their salvation. Unquestioning submission corrupts leaders and demeans followers. Making a cult of a leader is always a mistake. Fortunately hero worship generates its own antidote. "Every hero," said Emerson, "becomes a bore at last."

The signal benefit the great leaders confer is to embolden the rest of us to live according to our own best selves, to be active, insistent, and resolute in affirming our own sense of things. For great leaders attest to the reality of human freedom against the supposed inevitabilities of history. And they attest to the wisdom and power that may lie within the most unlikely of us, which is why Abraham Lincoln remains the supreme example of great leadership. A great leader, said Emerson, exhibits new possibilities to all humanity. "We feed on genius . . . . Great men exist that there may be greater men."

Great leaders, in short, justify themselves by emancipating and empowering their followers. So humanity struggles to master its destiny, remembering with Alexis de Tocqueville: "It is true that around every man a fatal circle is traced beyond which he cannot pass; but within the wide verge of that circle he is powerful and free; as it is with man, so with communities." ■

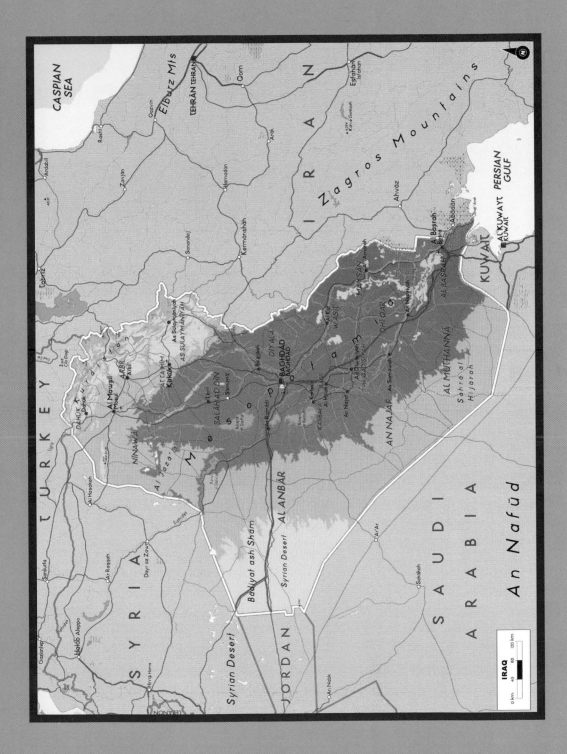

Saddam Hussein has been president of Iraq since 1979 and shows no signs of relinquishing his hold on the country, despite pressure from the international community since the Persian Gulf War in 1991. He employs biological and chemical weapons in battles, and many fear that Iraq is developing nuclear weapons as well.

1

"The Liberation of Kuwait has Begun"

We were looking out of our window, out of our fifth-floor room in the hotel, when a missile passed by on the line of the road on which the hotel stands . . . and it just went straight down the road. Where it was aimed for, I do not know.
—JOHN SIMPSON, BBC FOREIGN AFFAIRS EDITOR

S addam Hussein, President of Iraq, is known to his people by many names—the Anointed One, Glorious Leader, Direct Descendant of the Prophet, Chairman of the Revolutionary Council, field marshal of the armies, doctor of Iraq's laws, and great-uncle to all of Iraq's peoples. In public, Saddam wears a general's uniform decorated with medals and gold epaulets, even though he has never served in Iraq's armed forces. In his private life, he enjoys living in his many homes and palaces, each with its own swimming pool—a sign of wealth and success in a desert country like Iraq. In fact, Saddam's palace on an island in the Tigris River near Baghdad, the capital of Iraq, is adorned with gold doorknobs.

Fresh food is flown in for him twice a week. He eats lobster, shrimp, and fish. He makes sure to get plenty of fruit, vegetables, and dairy products, too. His food is prepared for him by European chefs, after it has been x-rayed and tested for poison. Sadly, these luxuries are enjoyed in spite of a United Nations study in 1999 that reported thousands of Iraqi children were dying of malnutrition.

Saddam also likes American literature, especially works by Ernest Hemingway like *The Old Man and the Sea*. He is even an author himself, and he has found the time in recent years to write two romances— *Zabibah and the King* and *The Fortified Castle*. His nineteen-volume official biography is required reading for Iraqi government officials.

In the evening, he likes to watch CNN, al-Jazeera (the Arabic cable station), and the BBC. He enjoys movies about intrigue: *The Day of the Jackal, The Conversation, Enemy of the State,* and *The Godfather*. A six-hour movie about his own life will be released soon in Iraq, edited by Terence Young, best known for directing three James Bond films.

There have been times, though, when things were not so good for the Anointed One.

On the night of January 16, 1991, B-52 bombers took off from the United States carrying conventionally armed air-launched cruise missiles. It would take them 11 hours to reach Baghdad. More than 160 U.S. aerial tankers orbited outside Iraqi early-warning radar range and refueled hundreds of aircraft. Shifts of RC-135, U-2RI, and TR-1 reconnaissance aircraft maintained 24-hour orbits to provide intelligence coverage. Powerful radars probed deep into Iraq. U.S. crews watched their glowing screens for Iraqi reactions.

On television, President George Bush announced, "The liberation of Kuwait has begun."

Five months earlier, on August 2, 1990, the Iraqi army had invaded and occupied Kuwait. A force of about 120,000 Iraqi soldiers and approximately 2,000 tanks and other armored vehicles met little resistance. The Kuwaiti army was not on the alert, and troops at their posts could not mount an effective defense. Some aircraft operating from southern Kuwait attacked Iraqi armored columns before their air base was overrun, and they sought refuge in Saudi Arabia. Of the 20,000 Kuwaiti troops, many were killed or captured, although up to 7,000 escaped into Saudi Arabia, along with about forty tanks. The United Nations had given Saddam Hussein until January 15 to withdraw from Kuwait.

Now, just hours after the deadline had passed, on board the warships of an international armada in the Persian Gulf region, pilots and flight crews prepared for the biggest air strike since World War II. On U.S. warships, sailors prepared Tomahawk land attack missiles (TLAMs) for their first combat launch. Shortly after midnight, several dozen streaked away into the darkness, headed for Baghdad at 700 mph and carrying explosive warheads weighing 1,000 pounds.

An hour later, while the TLAMs were still in flight, helicopters attacked early warning radar sites in southern Iraq. Stealth fighters had already passed over these sites en route to attack targets in western Iraq and Baghdad. The helicopters, cruise missiles, F-15E Eagle fighters, and British GR-1 Tornado fighter bombers tore gaps in Iraqi radar coverage for the smaller fighter aircraft which were follow-ing. At about 3 A.M. local time (7 P.M. EST) on January 17, a huge air armada led by a fighter sweep of F-15s and F-14s moved north from staging areas in Saudi Arabia toward Iraq. They took off in pairs, disappearing as they gained altitude. The aircraft were heavily loaded with bombs and under-wing fuel tanks for the long trip north. They also were armed with cannon and air-to-air missiles for self-defense.

At the Pentagon in Washington, D.C., planners were aware that each bomb could have a potential moral and political impact. Iraq has a rich cultural and religious heritage dating back several thousand years. Within its borders are sacred religious areas and thousands of archaeological sites that trace the evolution of modern civilization. To avoid damaging mosques, religious shrines, and archaeological sites, as well as civilian facilities and the civilian population, American military strategists, intelligence agencies, and the U.S. State Department had drawn up a joint no-fire target list. This list was a compilation of historical, archaeological, economic, religious and politically sensitive installations that could not be targeted. In addition, target intelligence analysts studied a six-mile area around each master attack list for schools, hospitals, and mosques to identify targets that required extreme care in planning. When targeting, if officers calculated the probability of collateral damage as too high, the target was added to the no-fire list.

Shortly before dawn, Baghdad residents heard explosions and saw flashes of light. CNN news presenters rushed out on to the balcony of their Baghdad hotel to broadcast live the start of the Persian Gulf War, or Operation Desert Storm.

What followed was a devastating and sustained aerial bombardment involving cruise missiles launched from U.S. warships and U.S., British, and Saudi Arabian fighter planes, bombers, and helicopters. More than 1,000 sorties were flown in the first 24 hours of Desert Storm. The main targets were military, but Baghdad, the Iraqi capital, was also heavily hit.

The 1991 Gulf War is often described as the first televised war. All over the world, television audiences were able to watch the war unfold on their television screens. Pictures of missiles launching and fighters taking off were broadcast daily. The devastating results of the bombing also made it onto television

The skies over Baghdad erupted with anti-aircraft fire as U.S. warplanes struck key Iraqi targets around the capital city on January 18, 1991. The Persian Gulf War had begun, prompted by Iraq's invasion and occupation of Kuwait.

screens. The daily briefings given by the allies used video footage and satellite pictures to show that military targets were being destroyed and that every effort was being made to avoid civilian casualties. Terms like "collateral damage" and "surgical strike" became part of the American vocabulary. In the capital city of Baghdad, military and communications installations were targeted, as well as the parliament, airport, defense ministry, and various palaces. All over the country allied aircraft hit major cities and military targets as well as Iraqi forces in Kuwait.

Iraq's retreat from Kuwait was halted by U.S. air-to-ground missiles on a highway just north of Kuwait City. This burned out convoy shows the devastating force of the March 1, 1991 attack.

By the end of February, the Iraqi army had made a desperate retreat from Kuwait. At a place called Mutla Ridge, thousands of Iraqi soldiers were pinned down in their vehicles as they tried to cross back into Iraq. Most were incinerated by air-to-ground missiles. A three-day ground offensive campaign ended on February 27, when U.S. President George Bush declared victory.

In his secret office, where he had been working during the 42-day war, Saddam called in one of his generals during the final days of the conflict to hear his assessment of Iraq's performance:

> "What is your evaluation, general?" Saddam asked.
>
> "I think this is the biggest defeat in military history," came the answer.
>
> "How can you say that?"
>
> "This is bigger than the defeat at Khorranshahr [one of the worst Iraqi losses in the war with Iran that cost tens of thousands of Iraqi lives]."
>
> Saddam said nothing for a moment. Then he replied, "that's your opinion."

A decade after the Persian Gulf War and the disastrous defeat of his military, Saddam Hussein continues a reign that has lasted more than 30 years. According to some estimates, in the third and fourth years of his formal rule (1981 and 1982) more than 3,000 Iraqis were executed. During the Iran-Iraq war, (1980–1988) Iraq suffered an estimated 375,000 casualties. Sixty thousand Iraqi soldiers were taken prisoner by the Iranians.

In major conflicts against his enemies, Saddam has authorized the use of chemical weapons. Weapons inspectors from the United Nations believe he has the capability to produce biological weapons such as anthrax, and perhaps even nuclear weapons. Since 1991, the United Nations has forced economic sanctions on Iraq until it agrees to allow inspectors to scour every square mile of the country in search of weapons of mass destruction.

Yet his defenders call him the leader of a sovereign nation who should not have to bow to international demands. In recent years, hundreds of groups around the world have called for a lifting of the sanctions against Iraq, calling them unjust and cruel.

These ruins are from the ancient Sumerian city of Ur in Iraq. The Sumerians were the first to cultivate land, use calendars, and may have invented the first written alphabet.

"He Who Confronts"

Because of lack of space the young spent most of their time
outside in the narrow, dirty, dung-filled alleys of their villages and towns.
They formed gangs, stole from farmers and from each other . . . This was
the fate which awaited Saddam, and these were the elements which
formed his early personality.
—SAÏD K. ABURISH
SADDAM HUSSEIN: THE POLITICS OF REVENGE

In ancient times Iraq was known as Mesopotamia, a name that
means "the land between the two rivers" (the Tigris and Euphrates
rivers). To the modern world, this region has become known as
the Cradle of Civilization.

The Sumerian culture flourished here around 4000 B.C. The
Sumerians were the first recorded people to cultivate land and use

calendars. The first written alphabet may have been invented here, too. The seat of Sumerian power was the city of Ur of the Chaldees.

Over many centuries, however, the Sumerians fought count-less invading enemies whose attacks took their toll on Sumerian civilization and culture. Fortunately, King Hammurabi of Babylon was able to salvage some of this civilization in 1700 B.C., and the region came to be known as Babylonia. On Hammurabi's death, the land fell under Assyrian rule for about two centuries. It was then restored to its former legendary glory under Nebuchadnezzar II, who built the famous Hanging Gardens and made Babylon the most celebrated (and notorious) city of the ancient world.

Various invaders conquered the land after Nebuchad-nezzar's death, including Cyrus the Great in 539 B.C. and the Macedonian emperor, Alexander the Great in 331 B.C. Then the armies of the Persian Empire overran Babylonia in the second century A.D. For 500 years, the region remained in Persian control until it was captured by Arab Muslims. The capital was moved to Baghdad. By the Middle Ages, Baghdad was a thriving commercial and cultural center—a city where humble marketplaces operated next to the walls of palaces and Eastern schools of religious thought.

In 1258 A.D., Mongol invaders from Asia sacked Baghdad and murdered the caliph (the term "caliph" means leader of Islam, or literally, the prophet Mohammed's successor). Baghdad stood at the center of a contest for supremacy that lasted 400 years, until the Turks conquered the region and added it to the Ottoman Empire in the 17th century. Turkish rule continued unchallenged until the end of the 19th century.

During World War I, Turkey became a German ally. The Ottoman Empire collapsed when British forces invaded Mesopotamia in 1917 and occupied Baghdad. At the Paris Peace Conference in 1919, the Allies (the coalition of the victorious nations in World War I) made Iraq—the territory encompassing the three former Ottoman provinces of Mosul, Baghdad, and Al Basrah—a Class A mandate. Under the mandate system, a territory that had formerly been held by Germany or the Ottoman Empire was placed under the supervision of the League of Nations. The responsibility for directly administering the mandate fell to Britain, which was keenly interested in the area's oil fields. Class A mandates were expected to achieve independence in a few years. In April 1920 the Allied governments confirmed British control of the region at a conference in San Remo, Italy. Local unrest, however, resulted in an Arab uprising in 1920 against British colonialism, and after costly attempts to quell it, the British government drew up a plan for an independent state of Iraq.

It was to be a kingdom, under the rule of Emir Faisal, and although the monarch was elected in 1921, full independence was not achieved until 1932 when the British Mandate was officially terminated. Iraq joined the League of Nations in October 1932 as an independent sovereign state. On Faisal's death in 1933, his son, King Ghazi I, succeeded him.

During this period of newly won independence and Iraqi nationalism, Saddam Hussein was born on April 28, 1937. His family were landless peasants who lived in the mud-hut village of Al-Awja on the outskirts of Tikrit, northwest of Baghdad. Saddam's name means "he who confronts." In accordance with Arab custom, Saddam's second name, Hussein, was his father's first name.

His father disappeared from the scene when Saddam was still only a few months old (the official version is that his father died.) His mother married a man named Hassan Ibrahim, nicknamed Hassan the Liar, who abused his small stepson with insults and blows. Forced to work like a hired hand, Saddam thrilled to a cousin's stories of what life was like attending school in Tikrit. His stepfather

Iraq achieved full independence from British rule in 1932, and the kingdom was ruled by Emir Faisal I. Saddam Hussein was born shortly after Iraq's independence, in 1937.

refused to allow him any schooling, however. At age 10, Saddam ran away one night to live in Baghdad with an uncle, Khairullah Tulfah, a devout Sunni Muslim who would later be governor of Baghdad. Khairullah was an Iraqi army officer, and passionate Iraqi nationalist opposed to the foreign interference. A popular pamphlet he wrote carried the title, "Three Whom God Should Not Have Created: Persians, Jews, and Flies." Khairullah became Saddam's hero.

That same year, 1947, Iraq entered the arena of international politics as a nation-player. Iraq bitterly objected to the United Nations decision to partition Palestine and sent several hundred recruits to the Palestine front when hostilities broke out on May 15, 1948. Iraq sent an additional 8,000 to 10,000 troops of the regular army during the course of the 1948 Arab-Israeli War. Fighting continued until the signing of a cease-fire agreement in May 1949.

But the Iraqis had arrived at the Palestine front poorly equipped and poorly trained. The humiliations they suffered on the battlefield reflected badly on the country's monarchy. The war also had a negative impact on the Iraqi economy. The government allocated 40 percent of available funds for the army and for Palestinian refugees. Oil royalties to Iraq were cut in half when the pipeline to Israel was shut off in 1948. The war and the lynching of a Jewish businessman led, moreover, to the departure of most of Iraq's prosperous Jewish community—about 120,000 Iraqi Jews emigrated to Israel between 1948 and 1952.

By the early 1950s, government revenues began to improve with the growth of the oil industry. The Iraqis constructed new pipelines to Tripoli, Lebanon, in 1949 and to Baniyas, Syria, in 1952. A new oil agreement, concluded in 1952, netted the government 50 percent of oil company profits before taxes. Government oil revenues suddenly increased almost four times over.

But little of the money was reaching the Iraqi people. Corruption among government officials increased; foreign oil companies employed relatively few Iraqis; and the oil boom had a severe inflationary effect on the economy. Inflation hurt in particular a growing number of urban poor and the salaried middle class.

Then, starting in 1955, the monarchy committed several foreign policy blunders that led to its undoing. The government announced that Iraq was joining a British-supported mutual defense pact with Iran, Pakistan, and Turkey. The Baghdad Pact constituted a direct challenge to Egyptian president Gamal Abdul Nasser. Nasser, a handsome, eloquent Egyptian nationalist, was expertly using the newly opened Suez Canal to make Egypt the most influential nation in the region.

In response to the pact, Nasser launched a heated media campaign that challenged the legitimacy of the Iraqi monarchy. He called on the Iraqi officer corps to overthrow it. Egypt then formed an alliance with Syria. In 1958 King Hussein of Jordan proposed a union of Arab monarchies to counter the Egyptian-Syrian union. Despite protests in the streets of Baghdad and other major cities, Iraq joined, giving the people the impression that the monarchy would do anything to preserve itself, even if it meant sacrificing the national interest.

At dawn on July 14, 1958, Iraqi officers of the 19th Brigade seized the government. The coup was triggered when Jordan's King Hussein, fearing that an anti-Western revolt in Beruit might spread to his country, requested Iraqi assistance. Instead of moving toward Jordan, however, an Iraqi battalion entered Baghdad and immediately proclaimed a new republic and the end of the old regime. The July 14 Revolution met virtually no opposition. The coup brought cheering crowds into the street calling for the death of the king. King Faisal II was executed, as were many others in the royal family. A mob attacked the British embassy and destroyed most of it.

An influential political organization involved in the coup was the Ba'ath party, to which Saddam's uncle had belonged for a number years. Saddam joined when he was 19 or 20.

During the 1950s, the Ba'ath was a secret anti-British political party, and its members were subject to arrest if their identities were discovered. From its early years, the

Iraqi Ba'ath recruited converts from a small number of college and high school students, intellectuals, and professionals— nearly all of whom were Baghdad Sunni Arabs, like Saddam's uncle, Khairullah Tulfah. A handful of Ba'ath high school students entered the Baghdad Military Academy, where they persuaded several classmates to join the party. In the 1957, the academy rejected Saddam, a devastating blow to his self-esteem, especially since he wanted to emulate his uncle.

This rejection may have prompted Saddam to volunteer for a murderous quasi-military operation two years later. The assignment was to assassinate Iraq's prime minister.

To the Ba'athists, the 1958 revolution was a disappointment. They had hoped that the new republican government would favor nationalist Arab causes, especially a union with Egypt. Instead, non-Ba'athist military officers dominated the government and did not support Arab unity or other Ba'ath principles. Some younger members of the party, including Saddam, became convinced that the Iraqi prime minister, Abdul Karim Kassem, had to be removed by force.

In October 1959 Saddam and a group of gunmen tried to kill the prime minister. Rushing up to a car carrying Kassem, Saddam and the assassins shouted political slogans while firing through the car windows. Incredibly, Kassem survived, but Saddam was shot in leg. With the help of party members, he fled to Damascus, Syria. Other Ba'athists were arrested and tried for treason.

In the spring of 1960, Saddam flew to Cairo, the capital of Egypt and the center of Arab nationalism. There, he enrolled in law school and became active in Cairo's regional Ba'ath party headquarters. He quickly rose up through the ranks. He also became engaged to his cousin Sajida, a schoolteacher and his uncle's daughter.

The Ba'ath party was forced underground again, biding its time until a second attempt to overthrow the prime minister, Abdul Kassem, was successful. In February 1963, Kassem was

Saddam Hussein was involved in two plots to remove Iraqi prime minister Abdul Karim Kassem, seen here in 1951. The second try was successful. But when Saddam's party lost power, he attempted to assassinate the cabinet and was arrested and imprisoned.

arrested and executed. A relative of Saddam's, General Ahmad Hassan al-Bakr, became prime minister.

However, the party's hold on power was shaky. The organization was small, its leadership was inexperienced, and it was not well represented in the officer corps or in the army at large.

Within nine months of taking power, all Ba'athists were expelled from the government. Saddam was then put in charge of the party's paramilitary arm and instructed to plan for another takeover the following year. The plan was for him to enter the Presidential Palace at the head of a commando team during a cabinet meeting and machine-gun the entire government.

On September 4, 1964, the day before the coup was to take place, the police uncovered the plot and sought Saddam's arrest. Refusing to flee a second time, he announced on the radio that he was still in Baghdad and defying capture. He was caught and imprisoned.

During the 18 months he spent in prison, Saddam was physically tortured. He was, however, allowed to receive visits from his wife. Tucked inside the clothes of his six-month-old son, Uday, were messages from fellow Ba'ath party members. In July 1966 while being escorted by guards to court, he asked permission to use the bathroom in a restaurant, and escaped through the back door.

His comrades happily welcomed him back and provided shelter for him. After all, there was much planning to be done. The Ba'athists were going to attempt one more violent takeover of the government, and Saddam would again play a key role.

After years of working behind the scenes in Iraqi politics—work that involved deceit and murder—Saddam Hussein became the president of Iraq in 1979. He quickly set his sights on ruling the Arab world.

3

Strongman

If a family was lucky, it produced a strongman, a patriarch,
who by guile, strength, or violence accumulated riches
for his clan. Saddam was now a strongman,
and his family was moving to claim the spoils.

—MARK BOWDEN

TALES OF THE TYRANT:
THE PRIVATE LIFE AND INNER WORLD OF SADDAM HUSSEIN

T he 1967 Arab-Israeli War ravaged the Middle East. In the
spring of 1967, the Israeli army provoked the Syrians into
firing on Israeli farmers, who had wandered into the Arab
demilitarized zone below the Golan Heights where the Jordan River
begins. Israel's provocation of the Syrian attack had political motives.
It allowed the Israelis to announce plans to march on Damascus, the

capital of Syria, to overthrow the Syrian government. The Israelis simultaneously provoked the Egyptians, another Arab nation, by claiming the Egyptians were too weak to come to Syria's aid. Conditions became ripe for conflict between the Israelis and Arabs.

President Nasser of Egypt responded by blockading Israel's southern port of Elat. Israel, claiming self-defense, attacked three Arab countries simultaneously in June. Within six days, the Israelis took control of the Sinai Peninsula, Syria's Golan Heights, and the West Bank in Jordan. They also occupied East Jerusalem, where the Dome of the Rock mosque is located. The Dome of the Rock is sacred to Muslims, as they believe it is the site of Muhammad's ascension into heaven. This site is equally important to Jews, as the mosque stands on top of Temple Mount, the remains of the Jewish temple destroyed by the Romans nearly 2,000 years ago. The one remaining wall, known as the Wailing Wall, is considered the holiest Jewish site. Therefore, for both Arabs and Jews, East Jerusalem has tremendous symbolic importance.

Outraged by Israel's successes, Iraq sent troops to fight the "Zionist entity," as those who oppose Israel's existence refer to the state of Israel. Once again, just as in the 1948 Arab-Israeli War, the Iraqis were trounced and forced to retreat.

For the Ba'ath party—strongly nationalist and pro-Arab— the defeat was unbearable, and many Iraqi citizens were disillusioned with the government regime responsible for the failure. This regime, led by Colonel Abd as Salaam Arif, came to power during the 1958 overthrow of the royal family. In 1963, when the Ba'ath party was expelled from the government after only nine months, Arif immediately announced that the armed forces would manage the country instead. The governing core consisted of Arif, his brother, and his trusted colleague Colonel Said Slaibi. Arif was both commander in chief of the armed forces and president of the republic. His brother was acting chief of staff, and Colonel Said was commander of the Baghdad garrison.

Iraqi president Arif relied on shaky military support to stay in power. After Iraq suffered a humiliating defeat at the hands of the Israelis, the stage was set for yet another coup on the Iraqi government.

Despite Arif's assurances to the Iraqis that the armed forces were strong enough to manage the country, the Iraqis were easily defeated when they came to the aid of their fellow Arabs. Moreover, Arif had never called for popular elections and was completely dependent on military support to stay in power. When the Ba'ath party persuaded four key officers that they could expect no honor supporting this regime, the stage was set for another coup. The four who agreed to cooperate were Colonel 'Abd ar-Razzaq an-Nayif, head of military intelligence, Colonel Ibrahim 'Abd ar-Rahman ad-Da'ud, chief of the Republican Guard, Colonel Sa'dun Ghaydan, and Colonel Hammad Shihab. An-Nayif agreed to cooperate on condition that he would be the new premier, and ad-Da'ud agreed if he would be appointed the minister of defense. The Ba'ath Party accepted this arrangement as a means to achieve power. But in private, the Ba'athists intended to dump their military co-conspirators at the earliest possible moment, for the party had little confidence in their loyalty.

After Saddam's escape from prison, he had been elected a member of the Ba'ath party's National Command. General Ahmad Hassan al-Bakr, who had briefly been Iraq's prime minister in the first Ba'ath takeover, was elected secretary general of the party. Saddam would serve as his deputy and run the Baghdad branch.

On the morning of July 17, 1968 Saddam rose at 2:30 A.M. to get an early start on a potentially bloody day. He began by bringing out all the weapons he had hidden in his house. His wife Sajida helped, as did their toddler son Uday, who ran around the room picking up grenades and handing them to his father like toys.

The conspirators met at Ahmad Hassan al-Bakr's house. Al-Bakr led the way in a white Mercedes; Saddam and the others followed in a truck. During the ride, Saddam changed into a lieutenant's uniform. When they reached the gates of the presidential palace, Colonel Ghayan dutifully made sure it was opened for them. A few minutes later, President Arif was awakened and informed that the army had revolted. He immediately surrendered and agreed to leave the country.

The first act of the new regime was to establish the Revolutionary Command Council (RCC), which assumed supreme authority. The RCC elected al-Bakr president of the republic, and he invited an-Nayif to form a cabinet. Saddam, at 31, was appointed vice-president. "Saddam's relatives in al-Awja were throwing their newly ascendant kinsman's name around, seizing farms, ordering people off their land," writes Mark Bowden in the *Atlantic Monthly* article "Tales of the Tyrant." "That was how things worked in villages. If a family was lucky, it produced a strongman, a patriarch, who by guile, strength, or violence accumulated riches for his clan. Saddam was now a strongman, and his family was moving to claim the spoils."

But almost immediately a struggle for power arose between the Ba'ath and Nayif-Da'ud groups. On the surface, the tension seemed to be about expanding socialism—a goal of the Ba'ath party—and foreign policy. But in fact the real issue was which of the two groups was to control the regime. Saddam settled the argument in characteristic fashion. On July 30, 1968, an-Nayif was invited to lunch at the presidential palace. After the meal, Saddam entered with a group of armed officers and told an-Nayif he was under arrest. It was agreed that an-Nayif's life would be spared if he left the country, and he was sent to Morocco as ambassador. In 1980, he was gunned down by Iraqi secret police in London. Ad-Da'ud, who was then on a mission to Jordan, was instructed to remain there. In *Republic of Fear: The Inside Story of Saddam's Iraq*, author Samir al-Khalil comments, "[O]ne can but stand in awe at the naïveté of officers like Nayef and Daud who played an important role in the overthrow of the [Arif] regime, had no intention of becoming Ba'athists, and actually believed Ba'athist promises."

Thus, the Ba'ath party finally came to be fully in control. But it faced a wide range of problems, such as ethnic and religious tensions, the stagnant condition of the economy, the inefficiency and the corruption of government, and the lack of political unity among Iraq's three main sociopolitical groups—the Shia Arabs, the Sunni Arabs, and the Kurds. Unity seemed unlikely, given that all three groups mistrusted one another. Occasionally, the Kurds burst into open revolt. And in the Middle East as a whole, Iraq wanted to challenge Egypt and Syria for the position of most influential country in the Arab world.

To move its agenda forward, the Ba'ath regime, in the style of countless dictatorships before and after it, launched a political campaign that harped on themes of disloyalty. Suddenly, the government was on the lookout for what it called "harmful pre-revolutionary values and practices." These included exploitation, social inequities, religious loyalties, apathy, and lack of civil spirit. Official statements called for abandoning traditional ways in favor of a new lifestyle. This new lifestyle embraced patriotism, national loyalty, collectivism, participation, selflessness, love of labor, and civic responsibility. These so-called "socialist principles and practices" would be instilled by the party's own example, through the state educational system, and through youth and other popular organizations. The Ba'athists particularly emphasized military training for youth. Such training was considered essential for creating "new men in the new society" and for defending the republic from the hostile forces of Zionism, imperialism, anti-Arab groups (e.g., from Iran), conservatives, opportunists, and reactionaries.

Less than two months after the Ba'ath party took control, an opportunity arose to demonstrate how "traitors" would be handled. A coalition of pro-Egyptians, Arif supporters, and conservatives from the military attempted another coup. Al-Bakr and Saddam punished them all between 1968 and 1973. Through a series of sham trials, executions, assassinations, and intimidations, the party ruthlessly eliminated any group or person suspected of challenging Ba'ath rule. On October 9, 1968, for example, the government announced that a major Zionist spy ring had been broken up in Basra. Seventeen Jews were flown to a military base in Baghdad and taken from there to a party interrogation center. President al-Bakr harangued the crowd for two hours, warning them about a "rabble of fifth columnists and the new supporters of America and Israel." Every so often al-Bakr shouted to the crowd, "What do you want?" And the answer would roar back, "Death to the spies, execution of the spies, all the spies, without delay!" Fourteen alleged plotters were publicly hanged, nine of them Iraqi Jews. Their bodies were left hanging in Baghdad's Liberation Square for more than a day as an example.

The Ba'athists also cemented their rule by formally issuing a Provisional Constitution in July 1970. This document, which is still mostly in effect, granted the party-dominated RCC extensive powers and declared that new RCC members must

Key leaders of the Ba'athist party, seen here at a military parade in 1969, quickly eliminated all opposition to their rule in the Iraqi government by intimidating and executing dissenters.

belong to the party's Regional Command—the top policy-making and executive body of the Ba'athist organization. In other words, no one who wasn't already deeply involved in the party would be allowed to join the top ranks.

In addition, the Ba'ath's ruling group was bound by close family and tribal ties. By 1977, Sunni Arabs from Saddam's hometown of Tikrit dominated it. Three of the five members of the Ba'ath's Revolutionary Command Council (RCC) were Tikritis; the remaining two members, al-Bakr and Hammad Shihab, were related to each other. The cabinet posts of president, prime minister, and defense minister went to Tikritis. Saddam was a key leader behind the scenes, and also a Tikriti and relative of al-Bakr. The leadership of the Ba'ath in 1968 also consisted almost entirely of military men. (Al-Bakr granted Saddam a generalship, although Saddam had never served in the military.)

However, only two men—Saddam and al-Bakr—really ran the party. Al-Bakr, who had been a leader with Arab nationalist causes for more than a decade, brought the party its popularity. Even more important, he could count on support from the army. Saddam Hussein, on the other hand, was a ruthless politician whose specialty was behind-the-scenes work. He was adept at outmaneuvering—and at times killing, if necessary—political opponents. Although al-Bakr was the older and more prestigious of the two, Saddam clearly had become the moving force (or threat) behind the power in Baghdad.

Beginning in the mid-1970s, however, al-Bakr was beset by illness and by a series of family tragedies. He increasingly turned over power to Saddam. The party committees, the intelligence mechanisms, and even ministers who formerly reported to al-Bakr were reporting to Saddam instead by 1977. Meanwhile, Saddam was less inclined to share power, and he viewed the cabinet and the RCC as his puppets.

On July 16, 1979, President al-Bakr resigned, and Saddam Hussein officially replaced him as president of the republic, secretary general of the Ba'ath Party Regional Command, chairman of the RCC, and commander in chief of the armed forces. Immediately, he plastered the walls of Baghdad with 20-foot-high posters of himself. Ominously, he had already seen to it that the party had built its own militia—50,000 soldiers who answered directly to him.

Saddam set out to consolidate his position at home by strengthening the economy. He pursued a state-sponsored industrial modernization program that tied an increasing number of Iraqis to the Ba'ath-controlled government. His economic policies were largely successful, in fact. They led to a wider distribution of wealth, to greater social mobility, to increased access to education and health care, and to the redistribution of land. Fueling his social reform programs was oil. Oil prices had quadrupled in 1973, when the Arab states had tried cornering the market. And in 1979, when the fundamentalist forces of the Ayatollah Khomeini brought down the Shah of Iran, Iranian oil production dried up. Iraq became one of the biggest oil suppliers in the world.

Among his early successes, Saddam had won the support of many Iraqis who had opposed the Ba'athists. In the United States, he tended to be seen as a stabilizer in a region that was volatile, especially after the Iranian revolutionaries seized 50 American hostages in the U.S. Embassy in Iran. Although he was strongly pro-Arab, his modernization programs, his stress on law and order, even his taste for tailored, Western-style suits created an image of a "modern Middle Easterner."

Success on the economic front spurred Saddam to pursue an ambitious foreign policy aimed at pushing Iraq to the forefront of the Arab world. Between 1975 and 1979, the success of his bid for power in the region hinged on improved relations with Iran, Saudi Arabia, and the smaller Gulf sheikhdoms. In 1975 Iraq established diplomatic relations with Sultan Qabus of Oman and extended several loans to him. The biggest boost to Saddam's quest for regional power, however, came from Egyptian president Anwar Sadat's signing the Camp David Accords in November 1978. If Egypt was prepared to make peace with Israel, then there was an opportunity for new leadership in the Arab world. Saddam eagerly stepped into the role.

He convened an Arab summit in Baghdad that denounced Sadat's reconciliation with Israel and imposed sanctions on Egypt. He also attempted to end his long-standing feud with Syrian President Hafiz al-Assad, and, in June 1979, Saddam became the first Iraqi head of state in twenty years to visit Jordan. In Amman, the capital of Jordan, Saddam concluded a number of agreements with King Hussein.

Closer to home, though, Kurdish unrest in the north continued to be a thorn in the side of the Ba'ath regime. Unlike most of the other religious and ethnic groups on Iraq, the Kurds remained fiercely independent. Their leader, Mustafa Barzani, maintained 15,000 Kurdish troops who were officially

These Kurdish troops were among the few Iraqis who maintained their independence from the Ba'athist regime that took over the Iraqi government. The Shah of Iran supported the Kurds in the fight against the Ba'athists, while the Soviet Union sided with the Iraqi government.

part of the Iraqi frontier force called the Pesh Merga, meaning "Those Who Face Death." In Baghdad, the Ba'athists were uncomfortable with a small ethnic army operating within their borders, but the legal status of the Kurdish territory remained unresolved. Until it was settled, the Kurds insisted on being well-armed. Saddam tried offering them the most comprehensive autonomy plan ever proposed. The Kurds regarded it coolly, and guerrilla attacks by Kurdish forces continued to erupt without warning.

In 1974, Saddam's patience with the Kurds wore out. In March, he attempted to have Barzani and his son assassinated. On the frontier, full-scale fighting broke out. When the Soviet Union agreed to side with Baghdad over the Kurdish question, the Ba'athists seemed to have Barzani and his men cut off. But the Shah of Iran, alarmed at growing Soviet influence in the region, promised military aid to the Kurds, with the full backing of the United States. When Iraqi forces reached Rawanduz and threatened to block the major Kurdish artery to Iran, the shah delivered a steady flow of military supplies to the rebels. Using antitank missiles and artillery obtained from Iran, as well as military aid from Syria and Israel, the Kurds inflicted heavy losses on the Iraqi forces. To avoid further defeat, Saddam Hussein sought an agreement with the Shah.

In Algiers on March 6, 1975, Saddam signed an agreement with the shah recognizing a number of Iranian boundary claims. In return, the shah agreed to prevent subversive (meaning Kurdish) elements from crossing the border. This agreement ended Iranian assistance to the Kurds.

Saddam signed, but inwardly he was seething. The Kurds had found allies in the United States and the Iranians, both non-Arabs (Iranians are not Arabian; they are Persian), sabotaging Saddam's visions of winning admiration throughout the Arab world. The intractable Kurds would pay.

Almost immediately after the signing of the Algiers Agreement, Iraqi forces went on the offensive and defeated the Pesh Merga, which was unable to hold out without Iranian support. Under an amnesty plan, about 70 percent of the Pesh Merga surrendered to the Iraqis. Some remained in the hills of Kurdistan to continue the fight, and about 30,000 crossed the border to Iran to join the civilian refugees, then estimated at between 100,000 and 200,000.

But in Saddam's mind, another guilty party still remained unpunished—Iran.

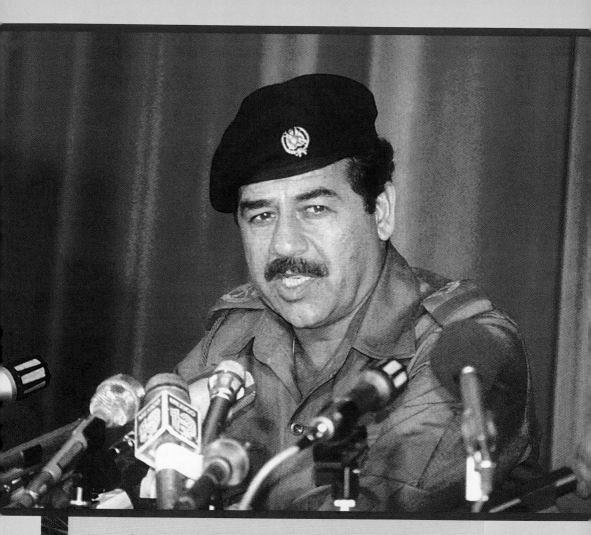

Iran and Iraq had engaged in many border clashes over the years. Iraq prepared to go to war over a dispute with Iran concerning a border outlined in a 1975 treaty. Saddam viewed the Iran-Iraq War that would follow as an opportunity to demonstrate Iraq's ability to dominate the Arab world.

4

The Iran-Iraq War

In March 1984, an East European journalist reported seeing
tens of thousands of Iranian children roped together in groups
of about twenty to prevent them from running away
as they attacked across minefields.

Saddam's years as a revolutionary with the Ba'ath party left him
keenly aware of the danger of dissent. In the Iraqi government,
he ousted his opponents and murdered dozens of other
government officials suspected of disloyalty. Among the Iraqi citizens,
he used chemical weapons to crush a Kurdish rebellion in northern
Iraq in the early 1980s. Beyond Iraq's borders, he invaded Iran in
1980, launching an eight-year war that ended in stalemate and left a
million people dead. All of these efforts were motivated by Saddam's
desire to rule the Arab world.

Of the many conflicts in progress around the world in early 1988, the Iran-Iraq War was by far the bloodiest and the costliest. Different issues fueled the Iran-Iraq War, including religious divisions, border disputes, and political differences. But above all, Iraq launched the war in an effort to replace Iran as the dominant Persian Gulf state.

Iraq and Iran had engaged in border clashes for decades. In 1979, an old dispute about the Shatt al Arab waterway flared up again. Iraq claimed the 185-mile channel up to the Iranian shore as its territory, while Iran insisted that the *thalweg*— a line running down the middle of the waterway—was the official border according to a 1975 treaty. The Iraqis, especially the Ba'ath leadership, regarded the 1975 treaty as merely a truce, not a final settlement. Saddam tore up the treaty in public, and the Ba'athists prepared to go to war.

They had every reason to be confident that Iraq would win. Not only did the Iranians lack leadership after the overthrow of the Shah in 1979 by Islamic fundamentalists, but the Iranian armed forces, according to Iraqi intelligence estimates, also lacked spare parts for their American-made equipment. Baghdad, on the other hand, possessed fully equipped and trained forces. Iraqi morale was running high. Against Iran's armed forces led by religious *mullahs* with little or no military experience, the Iraqis had twelve complete mechanized divisions, equipped with the latest Soviet weaponry. In addition, the area across the Shatt al Arab posed no major obstacles, particularly for an army equipped with Soviet river-crossing equipment.

For Iraqi planners, the only uncertainty was the fighting ability of the Iranian air force, equipped with sophisticated American-made aircraft left over from Shah of Iran's American-supported regime. Fundamentalist followers of the Ayatollah Khomeini had executed his key air force commanders and pilots. Nevertheless, the Iranian air force had displayed its might during local riots and demonstrations. It had also resisted the United States' attempt to rescue the

50 American hostages in the U.S. embassy in Tehran, the capital of Iran, in April 1980. This show of force had impressed Iraqi decision-makers. They decided to launch a massive, unexpected air strike on Iranian air bases in an effort similar to the one that Israel used during the 1967 Arab-Israeli War.

On September 22, 1980, formations of Iraqi Russian-made MiG-23s and MiG-21s attacked Iran's air bases at Mehrabad and Doshen-Tappen (both near Tehran), as well as bases at Tabriz, Bakhtaran, Ahvaz, Dezful, Urmia, Hamadan, Sanandaj, and Abadan. Iranian defenses were caught by surprise. But the Iraqi raids largely failed because Iranian jets were protected in specially strengthened hangars. Within hours, Iranian F-4 Phantoms took off from the same bases, successfully attacked strategically important targets close to major Iraqi cities, and returned home with few losses.

As the air war got underway, Iraq ordered six of its divisions across the border into Iran, where they drove as far as five miles inland and occupied 850 square miles of Iranian territory. By mid-October, a full division advanced through Khuzestan headed for Khorramshahr and Abadan and the strategic oil fields nearby.

Iraq's blitz-like assaults scattered and demoralized the Iranian forces. Many observers believed the Iraqis would win the war within a matter of weeks. In fact, Iraqi troops did capture the Shatt al Arab and also seized miles of Iranian territory. But the Iranians rejected a settlement offer and held the line against the militarily superior Iraqi force. They refused to accept defeat and slowly began a series of counterattacks in January 1981. Against Iraqi forces massed on the Karun River, Iran threw three "human wave" assaults into battle. Thousands of Basij (Popular Mobilization Army or People's Army) volunteers charged forward, many of them unarmed and picking up dropped weapons from fallen comrades. The recapture of Abadan, Iran's first major victory, came in September 1981.

Iraq used Soviet equipment, like T-55 and T-62 tanks, to stop Iranian attacks and push further into Iranian territory. Soviet- and French-made helicopters also helped the Iraqis inflict heavy damage on Iranian forces.

In March 1982, Iran launched its Operation Undeniable Victory, which marked a major turning point in the war. Iran broke through Iraq's "impenetrable" lines, split Iraq's forces, and forced them to retreat. In late June 1982, Iraq stated its willingness to negotiate a settlement of the war and to withdraw its forces from Iran. Iran refused and in July 1982 countered with Operation Ramadan on Iraqi territory, near Basra. Iran used elite forces and Basij volunteers in one of the biggest land battles since the end of World War II. Untrained combatants, some as young as nine years old, ran through Iraqi minefields and fortifications to clear safe paths for the tanks. Thousands died.

Near the end of 1982, Iraq received new Soviet equipment.

The ground war entered another phase. Iraq used newly acquired T-55 tanks and T-62 tanks, BM-21 Stalin Organ rocket launchers, and Mi-24 helicopter gunships to prepare a Soviet-type three-line defense that relied on obstacles, minefields, and fortified positions.

On February 6, 1983, Iran launched the first of three major human wave offensives along the frontier. Using 200,000 "last reserve" trained soldiers, Iran attacked about 185 miles southeast of Baghdad. Backed by air, armor, and artillery support, Iran's six-division thrust broke through. Iraq responded with massive air attacks. More than 6,000 Iranians were killed that day, while achieving only gains of a few hundred yards. In April 1983, Iraqi tank and infantry divisions stopped repeated Iranian attacks. Casualties were very high again, and by the end of 1983 an estimated 120,000 Iranians and 60,000 Iraqis had been killed. Except for the predictable attacks on important religious or historical anniversaries, the Iran-Iraq war became stalemated by the mid-1980s.

In early 1984, Iran launched another massive attack called Operation Dawn V. An estimated 500,000 troops (again, many of them volunteers) used shallow boats or traveled on foot to within a few miles of the strategic Basra-Baghdad waterway. Between February 29 and March 1, the two armies clashed and each sustained more than 25,000 fatalities in one of the largest battles of the war. Without armored and air support of their own, the Iranians faced Iraqi tanks, mortars, and helicopter gunships. Within a few weeks, Iran opened another front in the shallow lakes of the Hawizah Marshes, near the confluence of the Tigris and Euphrates rivers. Iraqi forces, using Soviet- and French-made helicopter gunships, inflicted heavy casualties on the Iranians.

Without sophisticated equipment to cut passages through enemy mine fields, Iran again resorted to the human wave tactic to break through Iraq's defenses. In March 1984, an East

European journalist reported seeing tens of thousands of Iranian children roped together in groups of about twenty to prevent them from running away as they attacked across minefields. An Iraqi officer who refused to mow down legions of charging Iranian teenagers was hauled up before Saddam himself. With onlookers watching, Saddam reportedly pulled out a revolver and shot him dead.

Within a four-week period between February and March 1984, the Iraqis reportedly killed 40,000 Iranians and lost 9,000 of their own men. But these statistics were unsatisfactory to Saddam. To raise the odds in his favor, he ordered the use of chemical weapons. Despite repeated Iraqi denials, between May 1981 and March 1984 Iran charged Iraq with use of chemical weapons some 40 times. Kurdish refugee camps in Iran were targeted to punish them for aiding the enemy.

In 1985, both sides tried a new strategy—shelling civilian centers and factories. Iraq began aircraft, long-range artillery, and surface-to-surface missile attacks on Tehran and on other major Iranian cities in May. Iran responded with its own air raids and missile attacks on Baghdad and other Iraqi cities. The only major ground offensive occurred in March 1985 near Basra, involving an estimated 60,000 Iranian troops. Both sides suffered heavy casualties.

In late March 1986, UN Secretary General Javier Perez de Cuellar formally accused Iraq of using chemical weapons against Iran. The secretary general called on Baghdad to end its violation of the 1925 Geneva Protocol on the use of chemical weapons, citing a report by four chemical warfare experts the UN had sent to Iran in February and March 1986. Iraq attempted to deny using chemicals, but the evidence was over-whelming. Hundreds of chemically burned victims had been flown to European hospitals for treatment. A British representative at the Conference on Disarmament in Geneva in July 1986 estimated that Iraqi chemical weapons had killed about 10,000 Iranians. In March 1988, Iraq was again charged with a major use of chemical warfare while retaking Halabjah, a Kurdish town in northeastern Iraq near the Iranian border.

On December 24, 1986, Iran began another assault on the Basra region. This "final offensive" resulted in more than 40,000 dead by mid-January 1987. Although the Iranian push came close to breaking Iraq's last line of defense east of Basra, they were unable to score a decisive breakthrough to win an outright victory.

By this stage of the war, both Iran and Iraq had lost most of their ships, but supplies continued to arrive on ships owned by other countries. Since 1981, both sides had engaged in the politically-dangerous practice of attacking ships of neutral nations. International newspapers dubbed this aspect of the Iran-Iraq conflict the Tanker War, named for oil tanker ships.

Iraq dramatically expanded the Tanker War by introducing French combat aircraft armed with high-tech Exocet missiles. Iraq's goal was to cut off Iran's oil exports and force it to the negotiating table. Iran retaliated by attacking a Kuwaiti oil tanker near Bahrain and then a Saudi tanker in Saudi waters five days later. The message was that if Iraq continued to interfere with Iran's shipping, then no Gulf state would be safe.

Gulf oil supplies to the rest of the world plummeted. Iraq and Iran would only accept a UN-sponsored moratorium, or temporary ban, on attacking civilian targets like ships. Later, Iran proposed an extension of the moratorium to include all Gulf shipping, but Iraqis rejected it unless the moratorium covered their Gulf ports, too.

As it turned out, the paper-signing ceremony for the moratorium was an empty gesture anyway. Iraq resumed attacking neutral ships soon after the agreement went into effect. In 1986 and 1987, Iraq stepped up air raids on tankers serving Iran and Iranian oil-exporting facilities, even vessels that belonged to the conservative Arab states of the Persian Gulf. Iran escalated its attacks on shipping in response.

Many of the neutral oil ships damaged or sunk were

Kuwaiti. The Kuwaiti government sought protection for its tankers from the international community in the fall of 1986. The Soviet Union responded first, agreeing to charter several Soviet tankers, which would fly the Soviet Union's flag, to Kuwait in early 1987. The United States hesitated to follow suit until May 17, 1987, when an Iraqi missile attack on the USS *Stark* killed 37 crew members. Iraq apologized and claimed that the attack was a mistake. Within a few weeks of the *Stark* incident, Iraq resumed its raids on tankers but moved its attacks farther south, near the Strait of Hormuz.

At this time, the citizens of the United States were against Iran, not Iraq. The Ayatollah Khomeini had made Iran an enemy of Americans when U.S. citizens were held hostage in the U.S. embassy in Tehran in 1980. The United States manipulated the *Stark* incident and used it to blame Iran for escalating the war and to send its warships to the Gulf to escort eleven Kuwaiti tankers that were "reflagged" with the American flag and refitted with American crews. Iran refrained from attacking the United States naval force directly. Instead, it used various forms of harassment, including floating mines, hit-and-run attacks by small patrol boats, and periodic stop-and-search operations. On several occasions, Tehran fired Chinese-made Silkworm missiles on Kuwaiti ships from the Al-Faw Peninsula. When Iranian forces hit the reflagged tanker *Sea Isle City* in October 1987, Washington retaliated by destroying an Iranian oil platform in the Rostam field. U.S. Navy Sea, Air, and Land (SEAL) commandos blew up a second one nearby.

In early 1988, the Gulf was a crowded theater of operations. At least ten Western navies and eight regional navies were patrolling the area, the site of weekly incidents in which merchant vessels were crippled. The Arab Ship Repair Yard in Bahrain and another one in Dubayy, United Arab Emirates (UAE), were unable to keep up with repairing damaged ships.

However, the war's end seemed inevitable when the Iraqis routed the Iranians in four major battles from April to August

Both Iran and Iraq attacked neutral oil tankers, many of them Kuwaiti, in attempts to cut off each other's supplies. To protect their oil interests, the Soviet Union and the United States offered protection to Kuwaiti tankers.

1988. In the first offensive, named Blessed Ramadhan, Iraqi Republican Guard and regular army units recaptured the Al-Faw Peninsula. The Iraqis punished their enemy with chemical weapons, using nerve and blister agents against Iranian command and control facilities, artillery positions, and logistics points. Then the Iraqis launched successful attacks on Iranian forces in the Fish Lake and Shalamjah areas near Al-Basrah, and recaptured the oil-rich Majnun Islands. Farther to the north, in the last major engagement before the August 1988 cease-fire, Iraqi armored and mechanized forces penetrated deep into Iran, defeating Iranian forces and capturing huge amounts of armor and artillery. In Baghdad, victorious Iraqi regiments displayed captured Iranian weapons amounting

This Iranian woman mourns at the grave of her son, who was killed in the Iran-Iraq War. The UN-established cease-fire put an end to the fighting between Iran and Iraq but did not resolve any of the issues that initiated the war.

to more than three-quarters of the Iranian armor inventory and almost half of its artillery pieces and armored personnel carriers.

Iran accepted United Nations Security Council Resolution 598, leading to an August 20, 1988 cease-fire. The Iran-Iraq war had lasted nearly eight years.

Casualty figures are unreliable, but estimates are that nearly a million people died, many more were wounded, and millions were made refugees. The Iraqis suffered an estimated 375,000 casualties, the equivalent of 5.6 million for a population like that of the United States. Another 60,000 were taken prisoner by the Iranians. Iran's losses may have included more than 1 million people killed or maimed. The war claimed at least 300,000 Iranian lives and injured more than 500,000, out of a total population of nearly 60 million.

Moreover, the war had resolved almost none of the issues that had brought Iraq and Iran to the battlefield in the first place. When the conflict ended, the conditions at the beginning of the war remained virtually unchanged. The UN-arranged cease-fire merely put an end to the fighting, leaving two isolated states to pursue an arms race with each other and with the other countries in the region.

Only one thing was clear. Saddam's military machine—numbering more than a million men with an extensive arsenal of chemical weapons, long-range Scud missiles, a large air force—emerged as the most powerful and battle-hardened armed force in the Persian Gulf region.

The Iraqi forces that crossed the border into Kuwait on August 2, 1991 met little resistance from the Kuwaitis. The UN called for an immediate withdrawal of Iraqi occupational forces, a demand that Saddam Hussein ignored.

5

The Persian Gulf War

The great, the jewel, and the mother of battles has begun.
—SADDAM HUSSEIN, JANUARY 6, 1991

Our strategy in going after this army is very simple.
First we are going to cut it off, and then we are going to kill it.
—U.S. GENERAL COLIN POWELL, JANUARY 21, 1991

The Iran-Iraq War had been a draw at the cost of a million lives. Saddam was bloodied, but not defeated. Despite its huge losses in the Iran-Iraq War, Iraq remained unchallenged as the most powerful military presence in the Gulf area. But a war machine like the one Saddam wanted to build—one that would make him feared throughout the region—required not only men and equipment, but cash and oil. Kuwait had both.

Britain's colonial rule of Kuwait ended in 1961 when the new country declared its independence. Iraq immediately wanted to attack Kuwait, arguing that prior to World War I it had belonged to Iraq under the Ottoman Empire. The Empire had indeed exercised a weak sovereignty over Kuwait in the late 19th century, but the British began protecting the area in 1899. In 1932 Iraq informally confirmed its border with Kuwait, which had previously been established by the British. When the Iraqis threatened to attack Kuwait in 1961, British troops and aircraft rushed back to Kuwait. A Saudi-led force of 3,000 from the League of Arab States (Arab League), which supported Kuwait against Iraqi pressure, soon replaced the British. In addition, to help resolve the border dispute, Iraq received a large compensation payment. Iraq finally recognized Kuwait's independence.

The agreement was short-lived, however. The boundary issue again arose when the Ba'ath Party came to power in Iraq after the 1963 revolution. The newly installed government officially recognized the independence of Kuwait and the boundaries Iraq had accepted in 1932. But when the Ba'ath party returned to power again in 1968, Iraq insisted that Bubiyan and Warbah Islands at the mouth of the Shatt al Arab waterway belonged to Iraq. Controlling the islands would give Iraq a highly desirable passage to the Persian Gulf. In 1973, Iraq amassed troops at the border near the Shatt al Arab.

In 1975 Saddam tried another approach. He proposed that Kuwait lease half of the Gulf islands under its jurisdiction—including Bubiyan, the largest—and surrender Warbah Island to Iraq. The Kuwaitis were outraged and rejected the proposal. In May 1981, Bahrain, Kuwait, Oman, Qatar, Saudi Arabia, and the United Arab Emirates banded together in the Gulf Cooperation Council to protect their interests and, if necessary, to defend themselves. Wealthy and oil-rich, but lacking significant military forces, they feared being plundered by Iraq.

Saddam continued to put pressure on Kuwait in the 1980s, wanting to build a naval base on Bubiyan Island. He also began accusing Kuwait of illegally siphoning off oil from Ar Rumaylah field, one of the world's largest oil pools, which Iraq and Kuwait shared. He threatened to use force against Arab oil producers, including Kuwait and the United Arab Emirates. They were conspiring with the United States, Saddam claimed, to strangle the Iraqi economy by flooding the market with low-priced oil. Expecting an Iraqi attack, Kuwait fortified itself.

In August 1988, Kuwait charged that a force of Iraqis backed by gunboats had attacked Bubiyan. United Nations investigators found that the Iraqis had come from fishing boats and had probably been scavenging for military supplies abandoned after the Iran-Iraq War. Kuwait was suspected of having exaggerated the incident to underscore its need for international support against ongoing Iraqi hostility. Kuwait was not crying "wolf."

The world was largely taken by surprise when the Iraqi army invaded and occupied Kuwait on August 2, 1990. An Iraqi force of about 120,000 soldiers and approximately 2,000 tanks and other armored vehicles met little resistance. The Kuwaiti army was not on the alert, and troops at their posts could not mount an effective defense. Some aircraft operating from southern Kuwait attacked Iraqi armored columns before their air base was overrun. Of the 20,000 Kuwaiti troops, many were killed or captured, although up to 7,000 escaped into Saudi Arabia, along with about forty tanks.

Having completed the occupation of Kuwait, the Iraqi armored and mechanized divisions and the elite Republican Guard advanced south toward Kuwait's border with Saudi Arabia. Intelligence sources indicated that the Iraqis were positioning themselves for a subsequent drive toward the Saudi oil fields and shipping terminals, possibly continuing toward

These Iraqi soldiers celebrate after the invasion of Kuwait. Saddam positioned Iraqi forces for a subsequent drive into Saudi Arabia, in an attempt to seize control of the world's oil supply.

the other Gulf states. Saddam was making a bid to control the world's oil supply.

On August 2, in the first of a series of resolutions condemning Iraq, the United Nations Security Council called for Iraq's unconditional and immediate withdrawal from Kuwait. Also on August 2, President Bush issued Executive Order 12722, "Blocking Iraqi Government Property and Prohibiting

Transactions with Iraq." Under this embargo, all Iraqi assets were frozen, and private financial transactions and trade with Iraq were prohibited. All direct U.S. exports and U.S. exports by third-party countries to Iraq were prohibited, except for certain informational materials and donations of articles needed to relieve human suffering, such as food, clothing, medicine, and medical supplies. The sanctions banned ordinary items like agricultural pesticides, children's bicycles, erasers, flour, soap, pencils, textbooks, shampoo, and toilet paper, among other items. On August 6, the United Nations formally voted to enforce an international embargo, which included forbidding member nations from purchasing Iraqi oil, a potentially hurtful blow to their economies. The media began referring to the United Nations embargo as the "Iraqi sanctions."

In response, Saddam defiantly proclaimed Kuwait as Iraq's 19th province. He ignored United Nations directives to retreat from Kuwait, proclaiming that "the great, the jewel, and the mother of battles has begun."

The United States prepared quickly to repel the invasion. On August 7, 1990, the Pentagon in Washington, DC began deploying troops. The next day President Bush ordered armed forces to Saudi Arabia. Their purpose was to protect the Saudi Arabians from any Iraqi attack. Iraq responded by declaring that male hostages would be used as human shields at strategic Iraqi sites to deter any military attacks on these locations. On August 22, 1990, Bush called up reservists. Iraq then announced that it would withdraw from Kuwait if it was allowed to retain the islands of Bubiyan and Warbah.

In the next few months, a coalition force of more than 600,000 ground, sea, and air force personnel was deployed to defend Saudi Arabia and to drive the Iraqis out of Kuwait. Called Operation Desert Shield, command of the force was divided. The commander-in-chief of the United States Central

Command, General H. Norman Schwarzkopf, headed United States, British, and French units. His Saudi counterpart, Lieutenant General Khalid ibn Sultan ibn Abd al-Aziz Al Saud, commanded units from 24 non-Western countries, including troops from Saudi Arabia, Egypt, Syria, Kuwait, and the other Gulf states. In addition to 20,000 Saudi troops and 7,000 Kuwaiti troops, an estimated 3,000 personnel from the other states of the Gulf Cooperation Council joined the land forces wing of the coalition offensive.

As Americans waited for an offensive to begin, rumors surfaced that Iraqis were stealing incubators from Kuwaiti hospitals, causing the deaths of infants. The Iraqi government countered by inviting a CNN tour of Kuwait. The group was promised access to several hospitals in Kuwait, but on the day of visit they were only allowed to see one hospital for a short time. Before CNN had time to file its report, the Iraqi government announced that the CNN news team found the reports of stolen incubators to be false.

In the meantime, however, Saddam prepared to play another card—environmental terrorism.

On October 26, 1990, *The London Financial Times* carried an interview with a senior engineer of the Kuwait Oil Company. He warned that Iraq had mined 300 of the 1,000 oil wells in Kuwait. If they exploded and burned, the effects could be disastrous. The Bush Administration, concerned about such a scenario, convened several top secret studies. The studies concluded that smoke from burning oil rigs would have little effect on weapons. On the other hand, estimates about the damage to the world's climate and the environment varied. The local impact was predicted to be potentially dangerous. Hospitals could be flooded with thousands of people suffering respiratory problems. In addition, "black rain" could damage crops and drinking water. Over the long term, global warming due to the increase of carbon monoxide was another possibility. One thing was clear: seizing the oilfields would be critical.

General Norman Schwarzkopf instructs troops in the Saudi Arabian desert in preparation for Operation Desert Storm. Schwarzkopf identified three targets: the Iraqi Republican Guard; Iraqi nuclear, chemical, and biological threats; and Saddam Hussein.

By November, General Schwarzkopf had identified three "centers of gravity," or necessary targets: Saddam Hussein; an Iraqi nuclear, biological, and chemical threat; and the Republican Guard, Iraq's elite troops. In December, U.S. troops were vaccinated in anticipation of biological warfare.

The Gulf arena would also be a new experience for many female U.S. soldiers. At first many units would not send females to staging areas in Saudi Arabia for fear of insulting the Islamic culture, which places women in a more passive role. Out of respect for their hosts, female soldiers were instructed to drive military vehicles only, keep their bodies covered, enter public buildings from the back door, and have a male companion accompany them in public.

The United Nations gave Iraq until January 15, 1991 to pull out of Kuwait. It did not. Operation Desert Shield officially became Desert Storm on January 16, 1991. President "Bosh," as some Iraqis called him because *bosh* means "nothing" in Arabic, began the bombardment with a vengeance. Hussein evoked the sympathy of his Muslim countrymen by describing the conflict as a *jihad*, or holy war.

Most Americans supported the Persian Gulf War. They sent parcels, letters, cards, and good wishes to the soldiers. They tied yellow ribbons around trees, displayed American flags, and proclaimed their patriotism with bumper stickers and T-shirts. Most Americans believed there were moral reasons to liberate Kuwait and establish a new world order with America as the only military superpower (the Soviet Union would dissolve in less than a year). However, not all Americans were in favor of the war. Anti-war demonstrations took place in the nation's capital and in several major cities. But on the whole, Americans wanted the Iraqis out of Kuwait.

Within only a few weeks of the first air attack on Baghdad on the night of January 17, coalition air forces had systematically destroyed electric power plants; water treatment facilities; telephone and radio exchanges; food processing, storage, and distribution facilities; transportation systems; and civilian factories. One of the most publicized of these incidents was the bombing of an infant milk factory that the United States said was a military factory. Saddam seized on the emotionally charged event, inviting tours of foreign journalists to see the destruction, because milk represents something essential to Arabic life. It symbolizes fertility, wealth, and life.

On February 13th, what became known as the Amirya bombing shook the U.S.-led alliance and brought home the human cost of Desert Storm. A U.S. stealth bomber dropped two laser-guided bombs on what the allies had mistakenly pinpointed as an important command and control bunker. Allied forces were unaware that hundreds of women and children had been routinely hiding in the bunker since the start of Desert Storm. The pilots had intended to drop the 1,800-pound bombs into the ventilation shafts of the shelter. One missed and exploded nearby, blocking the only escape route. The second plunged into the bunker and exploded in the middle of the largest room on the upper floor. The effect was terrible: 314 people are believed to have died, 130 of them children.

The scenes of badly burnt bodies being pulled out of the mangled shelter and distraught relatives waiting outside shocked the world. The bombing was quickly exploited by the Iraqi authorities, who allowed Western television crews to report the event uncensored.

On January 22, Iraq had begun oil tank fires in Kuwait in hopes of camouflaging troop movements. The number of burning oil wells would increase day after day until coalition troops seized the oilfields. In another gambit of environmental terrorism, Iraq deliberately dumped thousands of barrels of oil into the Persian Gulf on January 25, in an attempt to foul Saudi Arabia's desalinization plant.

Tensions continued to mount when Baghdad television displayed American pilots as prisoners of war. Saddam miscalculated the effect, however. Instead of encouraging the anti-war movement in the United States as he had hoped, broadcasting pictures of injured U.S. pilots seemed to harden American resolve. He further shocked the American public by attacking Israel with Scud missiles. The Bush administration quickly persuaded Israel not to retaliate for fear it would dissolve

Iraq set fire to many of its oil wells in an attempt to camouflage Iraqi troop movements. This tactic potentially had severe environmental implications, and may have contributed to Gulf War Syndrome suffered by U.S. soldiers.

the Arab alliance against Iraq. Instead, the United States ringed Israel with Patriot missiles capable of shooting down incoming Scuds.

When the massive coalition ground assault of Operation Desert Storm got under way on February 24, 1991, troops from the Persian Gulf states formed part of two Arab task forces. The first, the Joint Forces Command North, consisted of Egyptian, Saudi, Syrian, and Kuwaiti troops attacking Kuwait's western border. The second, Joint Forces Command East, consisted of about five brigades from Saudi Arabia, Kuwait, Bahrain, and Qatar which seized the Gulf coastline, immediately south of Kuwait. The main attack was a sweeping movement by United States, British, and French forces in the west designed to cut the links between the Iraqi forces in Kuwait and their bases in Iraq. Brigades from the Joint Forces Command North breached Iraqi defenses after allied bombing and engineer operations blasted passages.

On February 26th Saddam announced that Iraqi troops were withdrawing from Kuwait. Iraqi troops, although in strong positions, surrendered or streamed to the north. Units of Joint Forces Command East advanced up the coastal road, capturing the city of Kuwait on the third day of the offensive after light fighting and the surrender of thousands of Iraqi soldiers. In the two weeks that followed, thousands of Iraqi soldiers surrendered to American and other United Nations forces. Most were exhausted and eager to lay down their arms. Early on in the conflict, President Bush had decided that U.S. troops would not invade Iraq and capture Baghdad, a decision that many policy-makers have since questioned.

Abruptly, on March 3, 1991, Iraq agreed to all terms set up by the United Nations. U.S. Marines counted 22,308 Iraqi prisoners of war. On April 11, the United Nations Security Council announced that Desert Storm was over.

In total, the Persian Gulf War lasted 42 days and cost $60 billion, most of it paid for by the Saudis, the Japanese, and other coalition members. Not since the Spanish-American War, and perhaps never in its history, had the United States waged such a successful military campaign. Of the nation's 10 major wars, this one was the least costly in American lives. One hundred forty-eight Americans were killed in action, a body count far lower than commanders and strategists alike had anticipated. The American military, 20 years in the rebuilding after the debacle of Vietnam, displayed competence, valor, and extraordinary strength.

But U.S. personnel may have paid a price in unexpected ways, too. Upon returning from the Persian Gulf arena, some veterans complained of health problems—fatigue, headaches, memory loss, sleep apnea, chronic sinusitis, post-traumatic stress disorder, joint pain, rashes, backaches, and depression. These symptoms are now referred to as Gulf War Syndrome.

There are several theories relating to the possible causes of Gulf War Syndrome. One cause might be the toxins emitted from oil fires. Another cause might be chemical weaponry or fallout from coalition bombing. Although there is no irrefutable evidence that Iraq used chemical weapons, some tests conducted at the time showed the presence of toxins in the soil. A third theory is that the symptoms are a result of the vaccines used to deter the effects of chemical weapons and warfare.

The illness experienced by Gulf War veterans, the decision not to invade and occupy Iraq, and reports filtering out of Iraq as early as mid-1992 that Saddam's grip on power was as strong as ever—aided by frequent use of firing squads—raised several troubling questions. What was the true extent of Saddam's strength? Why was he not overthrown despite policies that had led to the death of hundreds of thousands of Iraqis? And did his military arsenal include chemical, biological, or even nuclear weapons?

This last concern preoccupied the minds of coalition leaders the most. In April 1991, as a condition for lifting the economic sanctions, the UN Security Council sought to eliminate Iraq's weapons of mass destruction—nuclear, biological, or chemical weapons and missiles with a range of more than 100 miles—by establishing the UN Special Commission on Iraq (UNSCOM). UNSCOM would also have the responsibility of ongoing monitoring and verification to prevent Iraq from re-acquiring the banned weapons from other countries.

As it turned out, however, the goals of UNSCOM turned out to be harder to accomplish than winning the Persian Gulf War itself.

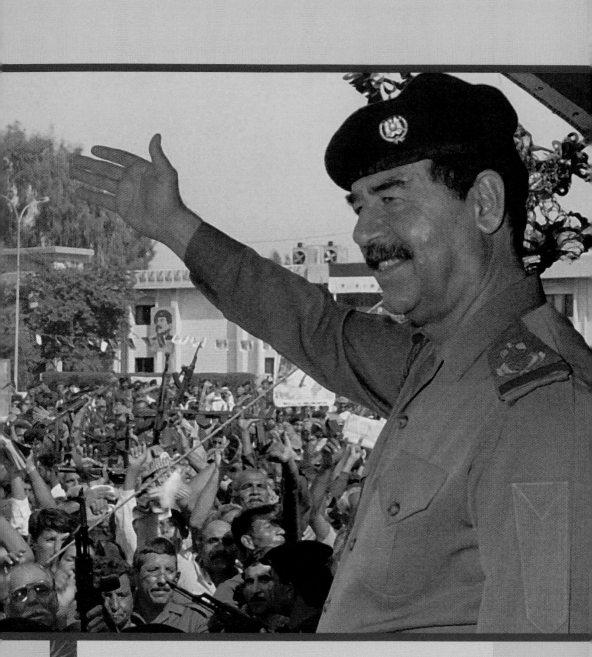

At one point, the U.S. hoped that Saddam Hussein would have a stabilizing effect on the turbulent political climate of Iraq. However, his tactics in the Persian Gulf War and his desire to dominate the Arab world quickly shattered that hope.

6

1992–1996: Tug of War

You Americans, you treat the Third World in the way
an Iraqi peasant treats his new bride.
Three days of honeymoon, and then it's off to the fields.
—SADDAM HUSSEIN, AT A 1985 MEETING
WITH U.S. STATE DEPARTMENT OFFICIALS

Any hope the United States had that Saddam Hussein might evolve into a dependable world leader evaporated with the Persian Gulf War. His power grab for the riches of Kuwait, coupled with his extravagant waste of human life and military resources during both the Iran-Iraq and Persian Gulf Wars, alarmed the international community. Moreover, he perversely took credit for everything that befell Iraq—good fortune and disaster alike—as if he wanted to imply that nothing ever really went awry in his regime.

According to him, all was going according to "plan." And to emphasize his infallibility, he executed his critics when they came within his reach. In an unmistakable statement of the United States' official opinion about his leadership qualities, U.S. planes dumped 21 bombs directly on Ba'ath party head-quarters on the final day of the Persian Gulf War. But Iraq's ruling clique, Saddam included, had long since evacuated.

Inside Iraq, signs of revolt against Saddam erupted periodi-cally. Perhaps, as the United States and its allies optimistically predicted when Gulf War hostilities ended in March 1991, he would fall suddenly from power at the hands of his own people.

During the 1970s, military officers unsuccessfully attempted to overthrow the Ba'athist regime on at least two occasions. In January 1970, an attempted coup led by two retired officers was discovered and thwarted as the conspirators entered the Republican Palace. A 1973 plot by Nazim Kazzar, a Shi'ite Muslim and the director of internal security, to assassinate President Ahmad Hassan al-Bakr and Saddam Hussein was also foiled. Kazzar, who resented both Sunni and Tikriti domination of the Ba'ath party, had taken a prominent part in organizing the massacre of communists in the chaos that followed the military takeover in February 1963. He had a reputation as a torturer. The old palace that he used as his headquarters was known as Qasr an Nihayah, the "Palace of the End." Few who entered ever came out, nor did their bodies receive public burial. When his coup plans failed, Kazzar fled toward the Iranian border. Before being apprehended, he killed the minister of defense, Hammad Shihab, who happened to be in the area inspecting border posts. Shortly afterward he was executed. Both coup attempts were followed by quick trials, executions, and purges of the armed forces.

The most serious attempt to assassinate Saddam occurred in 1982, after both a military defeat on the battlefield and a downturn in the economy. On July 11, 1982, the presidential party was traveling through the mixed Shi'ite-Sunni village of Ad Dujayl, about 45 miles northeast of Baghdad. Suddenly, it was surrounded by Shi'ite villagers and held for several hours before the army arrived. Subsequent reports revealed that a number of Saddam's bodyguards and some of the villagers were killed. As punishment, the Ba'ath government deported the villagers to Iran and destroyed their houses.

After the expulsion of Iraqi troops from Kuwait during the 1991 Persian Gulf War, President Bush encouraged the Iraqi people to revolt. The Kurds in the north and the Shi'ite Muslims in the south embraced Bush's encouragement. The largely Shi'ite south is a well of dissatisfaction with the Iraqi government. The Baghdad-centered Sunni Muslim population that supports Saddam Hussein's government has ignored their problems for 30 years. The Kurds' feelings of enmity towards Baghdad are long-standing, too. But when the Kurds and Shi'ites did rise up in late 1991, the U.S. failed to support them with military assistance. Iraqi troops crushed the southern Shi'ite uprising by strafing the marshlands where they live with helicopter gunships and shelling their villages. Kurdish refugees fled to Iran and Turkey.

To protect the Shi'ites from further attack, President Bush announced the creation of a "no-fly" zone on August 26, 1992. Accusing Saddam of using harsh repression to punish the southern Shi'ites, the United States, France, and Britain ordered the Iraqi military to stop flying planes and helicopters below the 32nd parallel—the southern third of Iraq. Allied warplanes patrolled the region, prepared to shoot down any Iraqi aircraft found in the zone. Though the measure was meant to last for only a few months, Britain and the United States were still enforcing it in mid-2003. Bush also cited the Iraqi government's continued blockade of food and medicine to the country's Kurdish minority in the north and executions of Iraqi dissidents as evidence that Saddam was defying UN Resolution 688. This resolution, passed at the end of the Persian Gulf War, prohibits the Iraqi government from repressing its own people.

In response, Iraq concentrated a considerable number of

combat aircraft at the 32nd parallel and announced it would counterattack if threatened.

The "no-fly" zone became a major military operation. The overall region encompasses about 47,520 square miles, roughly the size of Mississippi. The United States maintained substantial naval and air forces in the Persian Gulf region since the end of the Gulf War, including an all-purpose air wing of slightly more than 70 aircraft in Saudi Arabia. After Bush's announcement, the United States boosted its forces in the region with small numbers of additional planes, including RF-4G reconnaissance aircraft, RC-135 tankers, F-15C fighters, and EF-111 radar-jamming aircraft. The southern third of Iraq was divided into separate zones, each of which was monitored by AWACS radar planes capable of tracking hostile aircraft across thousands of square miles. Several combat aircraft—Air Force F-15s and F-16s, or Navy F-14s and F/A-18s—were assigned to each AWACS and challenged any Iraqi pilots who tried to penetrate the area. Britain pledged six Tornado fighters to the mission, and France several Mirage fighters. High-flying U-2 reconnaissance planes took photographs almost daily of Iraqi military positions on the ground.

When the "no-fly" zone restriction was announced, the 1992 American presidential election was only three months away. Democratic candidate Bill Clinton said he agreed with the measure. Six months into his own administration, after defeating Bush, Clinton demonstrated his commitment to keeping Saddam in check by pounding the headquarters of the Iraqi Intelligence Service with 23 Tomahawk missiles on June 26, 1993. What provoked the attack was the discovery of an Iraqi plot to assassinate President Bush during his visit to Kuwait the previous April. A 175-pound car bomb was supposed to go off by remote control when Bush visited Kuwait University. If all else failed, an assassin wearing a "bomb belt" would move near Bush and blow them both up.

From the decks of the destroyer USS *Peterson* in the Red Sea and the cruiser USS *Chancellorsville* in the Persian Gulf, the

Saddam Hussein retaliated harshly against a Shi'ite uprising in Iraq, which prompted the U.S., Britain, and France to set up a "no-fly" zone over the southern third of Iraq. This U.S. F-16 patrols the "no-fly" zone.

23 Tomahawk cruise missiles flew for two hours before smashing into the Iraqi Intelligence Service in downtown Baghdad. The missiles, which cost an estimated $1.1 million each, typically fly 50 to 100 feet above the ground and navigate by radar according to detailed maps stored in onboard computers. Each missile is capable of carrying up to 1,000 pounds of conventional explosives. Though the attack was scheduled for shortly before dawn to minimize casualties, and Tomahawks are said to be accurate to within one yard, Iraq reported that the missiles missed their target and hit a residential area instead. Reporters were not allowed in the area to confirm these claims.

By November 1994, it looked as if the combination of military retaliation and United Nations economic sanctions against Iraq was working. On November 10, Iraq recognized the sovereignty of Kuwait and accepted the border between the two nations drawn in 1993 by a United Nations commission. The Security Council debated whether the action was enough to lift the sanctions. All 15 council nations had insisted on Iraq's recognition of Kuwait as one condition for lifting the ban on commercial exports that prevented Iraq from selling its oil abroad, which was crippling its economy. Russia pledged to work in the Security Council to lift the oil embargo if Iraq would renounce its claims to Kuwait and cooperate fully with a UNSCOM team overseeing the dismantling of its weapons of mass destruction. Russia had recently signed a $10 billion economic cooperation agreement with Iraq that would take effect after the sanctions were lifted, and France had been negotiating new oil contracts.

On April 14, 1995, the UN Security Council passed a resolution allowing the partial resumption of Iraq's oil exports to buy food and medicine (later called the "oil-for-food program"). Reluctantly, Iraq officially accepted the following month that only some of the sanctions would be lifted. In October, Saddam won a referendum that extended his presidency for another seven years.

But then in late summer, as if impatient with the restraints imposed by the United Nations and the "no-fly" zone, the Iraqi leader attempted to break out of his confinement.

On August 31, Saddam defied U.S. warnings and sent 30,000 soldiers and three armored columns into a northern Kurdish stronghold, overrunning the city of Irbil. A Baghdad government spokesman announced Iraqi forces would withdraw once new authorities had been installed in Irbil. With Iraq's swift assault on the Kurds, Saddam disobeyed the United States for the first time since 1991. He propelled his forces into an area of Iraq populated by the 3.5 million Kurds, which the U.S.-led forces were pledged to assist. Iraq claimed it had invaded at the invitation of Kurdish leader Massoud Barzani, who had been feuding for control with archrival Jalal Talabani, whose group had recently received help from Iran. Iraq warned the United States to keep out of its Kurdish north, vowing to turn the area into another Vietnam if Washington intervened.

Saddam violated a UN resolution and U.S. warnings when he sent Iraqi troops into Irbil to attack a Kurdish stronghold. The U.S. responded by sending warships and firing cruise missiles against Iraqi air defenses.

But President Clinton and Washington officials maintained that Iraq's seizure of Irbil violated UN Resolution 688, which condemned Saddam's suppression of the Kurds and demanded the Iraqi leader respect the human and political rights of all his country's citizens. On September 3, 1995, U.S. warships fired a volley of 27 cruise missiles against air defenses in southern Iraq and followed it up with a second round of 17 missiles the next day. Saddam responded angrily, urging his air force and anti-aircraft gunners to attack U.S. and allied planes in the "no-fly" zone.

But in fact Saddam's retaliation never came during the next two years, except in occasional skirmishes between Iraqi forces and U.S. and British fighters. (France had eased out of its commitment to enforce the zone). Instead, realizing that he would lose a military face-off between his government and the United Nations, Saddam changed tactics in April 1991, the month after the Persian Gulf War ended. He challenged his enemies to a contest of wills—the weapons inspection game.

Rolf Ekeus led the UN Special Commissions on Disarmament of Iraq, and reported on Iraq's deliberate attempts to mislead UN weapons inspectors. It became clear that Saddam Hussein was not going to comply with UN demands without a fight.

7

The Weapons Inspection Game

Iraq stated that no documents existed in Iraq because
they had been destroyed. That was exploded totally, because
Iraq itself admitted in writing even that it had been lying,
cheating systematically from when we started in 1991
up until this very date in August of 1995.
—SWEDISH DIPLOMAT ROLF EKEUS,
FORMER HEAD OF THE UN WEAPONS INSPECTION TEAM

President Bush had resisted the temptation to follow Saddam's retreating armies into Iraq. The goal of the Persian Gulf War was to drive the invaders out of Kuwait and back inside their own borders. With this accomplished in 46 days, coalition armies watched as the remnants of Iraq's forces traveled north toward home. But the restraint shown by the United States and its allies left open a sinister possibility—that Iraq still had unused weapons of mass

destruction, or the capabilities for making them.

Exactly one month after the cessation of hostilities, on April 3, 1991, the United Nations passed Resolution 687 creating the UN Special Commission on Iraq (UNSCOM). The resolution made clear that as a condition for lifting the economic sanctions, Iraq would have to accept, under international supervision, the destruction, removal, or rendering harmless of its weapons of mass destruction, ballistic missiles with a range over 100 miles, and related production facilities and equipment. It also provided for ongoing monitoring and verification of Iraq's compliance with the ban on these weapons and missiles. On April 6, Iraq formally agreed to allowing UNSCOM inspection teams inside its borders. Two months later, the first contingent arrived.

Almost immediately, Iraq dug in its heels. Only three weeks into inspections, a UNSCOM team attempted to intercept Iraqi vehicles carrying nuclear-related equipment. Iraqi personnel fired warning shots in the air to prevent the inspectors from approaching the vehicles. Although the equipment was later seized and destroyed under international supervision, the warning shots fired were symbolic. Saddam's government would not cooperate without a fight. A new contest had begun.

Every few months, reports by Swedish diplomat Rolf Ekeus, who led the UN investigations from the cease-fire through the summer of 1997, spoke of gaps and inconsistencies, incorrect information, and deliberate attempts to mislead the UNSCOM teams. Periodically, Iraq's Deputy Prime Minister Tariq Aziz would counter by regularly asserting that Iraq was complying with the inspections.

By 1994, after three years' work, UN inspectors had accounted for most of Iraq's remaining nuclear and missile capacity. But they still knew little about Saddam Hussein's chemical weapons—and almost nothing about his ability to wage biological warfare. Resources for chemical weapons, which kill through exposure to poisons like toxic gas, are not hard for specialists to detect. But biological weapons spread death through infectious disease, and these deadly organisms are inexpensive to make with simple equipment. A factory that supposedly makes yeast for bread could just as easily be growing the bacteria for anthrax. That was the concern UN biologists had in mind, for instance, when they visited the Al-Hakam protein plant southwest of Baghdad in June 1994.

Their first disturbing impression was that the plant was enormous. Great quantities of protein can be grown in small spaces. What was the purpose of the tangle of pipes, funnels, heating units, and conveyors? A second mystery surfaced when closer examination revealed rows of steel drums containing a powder called growth medium—a plant food for organisms grown in fermenters. Growth medium is needed to produce protein, but it is also essential to manufacturing biological weapons. The inspectors estimated that Iraq would need about one ton of growth medium per year. The total amount in the steel drums was 34 tons.

The UNSCOM team concluded that the Al-Hakam plant was making anthrax, one of nature's deadliest organisms. Anthrax can kill a person in 48 hours. The inspectors blew up the plant. When team leader Ekeus questioned Iraqis about what they were planning to do such large quantities of anthrax, the reply was that the decision was to make it— how to use it would be decided later.

Between May 1992 and September of 1997, Iraq gave the United Nations seven reports, declaring that each was a full, final, and complete disclosure of its biological warfare program. The United Nations rejected all of them as not even remotely credible.

Nevertheless, until the mid-1990s critics reviewed Ekeus' reports skeptically, believing that a recently defeated

UN inspectors discovered 34 tons of growth medium in an Iraqi plant, which was being used to create anthrax used in biological weapons. These inspectors seized the media and supervised its destruction.

Iraq could not have the resources to make weapons of mass destruction. Where would the resources for nuclear weapons come from, for instance?

Then, in 1995, Saddam's son-in-law, Hussein Kamel, defected from Iraq to Jordan. For the first time, UN member nations began to grasp how much destructive potential Iraq was still concealing. Hussein Kamel told officials that Iraq had obtained enriched uranium, used in manufacturing nuclear weapons, from France and Russia.

Days after Hussein Kamel's announcement, even bigger revelations surfaced from a bizarre episode. Boxes of secret Iraqi documents turned up on a Baghdad chicken farm. Until then, the Iraqi government had insisted it had no documents relating to weapons of mass destruction because there were no such programs. But the "chicken farm stash" was a collection of memoranda stating the opposite.

"Iraq stated that they had declared everything," Ekeus told CNN. "Iraq stated that no documents existed in Iraq because they had been destroyed. That was exploded totally, because Iraq itself admitted, in writing even, that it had been lying, cheating systematically from when we started in 1991 up until this very date in August of 1995."

In 1997, UNSCOM stepped up its efforts, certain that somewhere hidden biological warfare programs were continuing, probably under the guise of pharmaceutical or food production. "Concealment teams" were created to follow suspicious individuals and pinpoint locations of possible hiding places. The move stiffened Iraqi resistance. For example, when a concealment team was using a helicopter for scouting, Iraqi representatives on board became hostile. They fought with the photographer, tried to grab the flight controls, and threatened to shut off the fuel system. Other Iraqi helicopters swung in close, causing a near-collision. Saddam, growing impatient with the cat-and-mouse game, tried outright intimidation.

On November 2, 1997, the Iraqi government warned the United States to halt its U-2 reconnaissance flights over the country or Iraq would use anti-aircraft weapons to protect its airspace. Two weeks later, Iraq expelled six members of the UN inspection team. The UN Security Council advised them to leave for Jordan. Meanwhile, President Clinton met with his security advisers to decide on a response that would make clear that the United States was determined to carry through its mission. France, Russia, China, and Egypt expressed that they were strongly opposed to the use of force. Abruptly, at the end of November, the Iraqis agreed to allow the Americans to return.

By December, however, inspections had again ground to a halt. Australian ambassador Richard Butler, who was now in charge of the weapons inspection, told the UN that his talks with Iraqi officials on dismantling Baghdad's weapons of mass destruction had made little headway. As if to emphasize the Iraqi government's refusal to cooperate any further, Iraqi anti-aircraft batteries fired on British and American planes patrolling the "no-fly" zone. The jets destroyed the installations with air-to-ground missiles. On October 31, 1998, Iraq ended all forms of cooperation with UNSCOM.

By early December of that year, the weariness over trying to get Iraq to comply with the terms of the UN resolution had spread to the Security Council. France, Russia, and China—three of the five permanent members of the council—voted to end the economic sanctions on Iraq and to reorganize UNSCOM. Britain and United States threatened to veto the move (Security Council measures require a unanimous vote), fearing a watered-down commission.

Before a showdown in the UN could occur, the United States effectively ended the debate. On the nights of December 16 through 18, U.S. warships fired 200 cruise missiles at Iraqi air fields, chemical plants, missile production and storage facilities, air defense systems, and surface-to-air missile sites. President Clinton indicated that at least one major aim was to punish Saddam Hussein for not fully cooperating with UN weapons inspectors.

But if the U.S., with lukewarm support of the Security

In the oil-for-food program, Iraq was permitted to sell oil at market prices under contracts approved by the UN. The funds from the sale of this oil were put into an escrow account and used to buy food and medicine for Iraqi citizens.

Council and Arab nations, was using a "big stick" approach in trying to discipline Iraq with military attacks, it was also continuing to support a diplomatic approach—the oil-for-food program. Under the program, Iraq is allowed to sell oil at market prices under contracts approved by the United Nations, with all revenue going into a UN escrow account. Those funds—a maximum of $10.5 billion a year—are then used to import food, medicine, and other humanitarian supplies through contracts approved by a UN committee made up of representatives of all Security Council countries. A Security Council member can veto any contract or ask that a contract be put on hold pending further investigation, if it believes the goods are not for legitimate humanitarian purposes.

By the late 1990s, however, the economic sanctions were finding less and less support. According to the UN Children's Fund (UNICEF) report in 1999, some 500,000 Iraqi children had died from malnutrition or lack of medical attention since sanctions were imposed after Iraq invaded Kuwait in 1990. Although the UNICEF report took pains to spread the blame for increased mortality on economic sacrifices the Iraq government had made to support its war efforts, major news organizations equated sanctions with causing children's deaths.

Two U.S.-based groups of doctors expressed their anger over these sanctions by traveling illegally to Iraq. Risking as much as 12 years in prison and $50,000 in fines, the doctors from the Chicago-based group Voices in the Wilderness and the Seattle-based Physicians for Social Responsibility personally delivered medical supplies and textbooks to Baghdad University Medical School and hospitals. Dozens of Internet sites manned by student groups, humanitarian groups, and peace activists had appeared by 1999, calling for an end to sanctions as an ineffective and cruel means to forcing weapons inspections inside Iraq. In 2000, the Baghdad airport reopened and dozens of humanitarian flights began arriving from various countries and international organizations.

However, Saddam was not above using the oil-for-food program to achieve his political ends by increasing his people's suffering, either. On April 8, 2002, Iraq suspended oil shipments to protest Israeli military incursions into the West Bank of Palestine. By April 30, funds used by the UN to purchase humanitarian goods had dried up. The U.S. State

Department estimated that the suspension had resulted in a loss of $1.2 million in sales of oil that could have been used to purchase humanitarian supplies.

On May 3, after the Israelis had begun pullbacks from Palestinian areas, the Iraqi government began selling oil again.

In his January 2002 State of the Union Address, President Bush spoke of an "axis of evil" that included Iran, North Korea, and Iraq. Among the offenses Bush cited in this speech were Iraq's failure to comply with weapons inspectors and its development of weapons of mass destruction.

8

A Regime Change in Baghdad

He's a problem, and we're going to deal with him.
–U.S. President George W. Bush, speaking about Saddam Hussein,
***The Chicago Tribune,* April 9, 2002**

After the Persian Gulf War in 1991, the UN Security Council established UNSCOM to oversee the destruction of Iraq's stockpiles of chemical and biological weapons and ballistic missiles. But although UNSCOM did have some success, it closed its center in Baghdad in December 1998 for lack of cooperation. Air strikes began by the United States and Great Britain. A year later, over Iraq's objections, the UN Security Council created UNMOVIC (the United Nations Monitoring, Verification, and Inspection Commission) to replace UNSCOM and to "establish and operate a reinforced, ongoing monitoring and verification system, address unresolved disarmament issues, and identify additional sites to be covered by the new monitoring system." The purpose of UNMOVIC was to enable the UN to lift the crippling economic sanctions it had placed on Iraq; if UNMOVIC could show that Iraq had cooperated fully with inspections for 120 days, then the UN would tentatively lift the sanctions.

It took almost three years for the members of UNMOVIC to be chosen, approved, and trained and for a dialogue to begin with Iraq. Under international pressure, Saddam readmitted weapons inspectors in September 2002. The team of UN inspectors currently combing Iraq aims to determine how Saddam's stockpile has changed since inspectors were pushed out in 1998—specifically, what has become of all the chemical and biological weapons that Iraq is known to have produced and whether Iraq has assembled a program in nuclear weapons.

There can be no doubt that Iraq has misled inspectors about its biological weapons program. It has alternately claimed to have destroyed its program completely and denied having such a program at all. In 1995, Iraq admitted to having offensive biological warfare capability, though it had insisted before that its program was for purely defensive research. It finally declared some 33,000 liters of biological agents, as well as delivery systems, including Scud missile warheads and aerial bombs and dispensers, that it had prepared for use in the Gulf War. The destruction of these has never been verified. Iraq may still be hiding thousands of liters of growth media, a precursor to biological agents. Thousands of munitions remain unaccounted for, too, including as many as 25,000 rockets and 15,000 artillery shells. In theory, Iraq has had no missiles since the Gulf War, but as late as 2002 Iraq built at least one new testing bed and facilities for producing rockets and processing rocket fuel.

There is also no question that Iraq has had a chemical program. In fact, it is one of the few countries to have deployed chemical agents successfully. Saddam used mustard gas and nerve gases against Iranians and Iraqi Kurds at least ten times between 1983 and 1988. In 1986, his deployment of nerve and mustard gases in the Al-Faw peninsula killed 8,000 Iranians, and his nerve gas attacks in 1989 killed 5,000 Kurds. Some 30,000 Iranians who were exposed to mustard gas during the Iran–Iraq War (1980–1988) are *still* being treated for their injuries. Although Saddam claims to have stopped production of chemical weapons, he may actually be reviving the program: at least three key Iraqi chemical centers whose products can be used to make weapons were constructed or modified in 2002. By the best estimates available, even the revised declaration of December 2002 may have failed to list up to 600 metric tons of weaponized chemical agents, including mustard gas and nerve agents.

Of greater concern, though, is the possibility that Iraq is developing nuclear weapons. The Bush administration has accused Saddam of trying to import some 60,000 aluminum tubes that, among other uses, can be used to produce weapons-grade uranium. Also, Iraq attempted to purchase uranium from Niger in the mid-1980s, and, though both Iraq and Niger say the attempt was unsuccessful, Iraq did not report this in its most recent declaration. (Iraq has further claimed that this was not uranium but uranium *oxide*—not itself a weapon, but a source of uranium—and that the 2002 declaration included this.) It has been estimated that Iraq could achieve nuclear capability in as little as two to five years, depending on whether it was helped by other nations.

It has also been suggested that Saddam has a history of supporting extremist groups. In August 1998, the United States bombed a pharmaceutical factory in Khartoum in retaliation for bombings of the American embassies in Kenya and Tanzania, and U.S. officials later announced their belief that Iraqi scientists had used that factory to develop nerve gases for use by terrorists. The Bush administration has tried repeatedly to link Saddam to Al Qaeda, and there can be little doubt that his resources have supported anti-U.S. groups in one way or another. Any chemical, biological, or nuclear stockpiles left in his power could easily fall into even more dangerous hands.

Furthermore, Saddam's record of human rights violations has outraged the international community. He forcibly relocated around 150,000 Marsh Arabs of southern Iraq by draining the marshes in which they lived. He controls all the Iraqi media and has a legendary record of dealing brutally with dissent against his rule; decrees of the Revolutionary Command Council (RCC) even give state institutions the power to suppress political opponents. The UN Commission on Human Rights issued a resolution on April 19, 2002 that condemned "the systematic, widespread and extremely grave violations of human rights and of international humanitarian law by the Government of Iraq, resulting in an all-pervasive repression and oppression sustained by broad-based discrimination and widespread terror." British Foreign Secretary Jack Straw released a report on December 2, 2002 that described Iraqi violations of human rights, aiming to help the world to understand "the comprehensive evil that is Saddam Hussein." The report contained accounts by survivors of Saddam's abuses, including various extreme forms of torture and execution. Estimates claim that up to 15 percent of Iraq's population— some three or four million people—have fled the country, rather than live under Saddam's rule. As of mid-2000, amputation of the tongue was approved by the RCC for dissenters, even though Iraqi law explicitly forbids torture.

Even though the first President Bush did not oust Saddam in the first Gulf War, the United States clearly decided years ago to end Saddam's reign. The Iraq Liberation Act of 1998, signed by President Clinton, established a U.S. policy of supporting "those elements of the Iraqi opposition that advocate a very different future for Iraq than the bitter reality of internal repression and external aggression that the current regime in Baghdad now offers." The act was followed by approximately $96 million in financial support to groups that opposed Saddam, along with military equipment and training. The current Bush administration not only has continued this support, but also means to use military force to effect a "regime change" in Baghdad.

In his State of the Union Address in January 2002, President George W. Bush spoke of an "axis of evil" consisting of Iran, North Korea, and Iraq. He summarized his case against Iraq in one broad paragraph: Iraq had (1) supported terrorist groups and flaunted its hostility toward the United States, (2) worked to develop anthrax, nerve gases, and nuclear weapons for over a decade, (3) used poison gas to murder thousands of its own citizens, and (4) agreed to international inspections and then expelled the inspectors—presumably because it had something to hide.

After the UN's condemnation of Iraq's human rights violations in April, seen as a sign of UN support, the Bush administration began to build an international coalition to support the forcible removal of Saddam Hussein. An initial push failed to establish widespread European support—a pattern that would continue—so President Bush spent May 2002 working subtly in Germany and Russia, making his point without ever referring directly to Iraq. Prime Minister Tony Blair of Great Britain emerged as a key link between the United States and Europe and the chief American ally in the question of military intervention. The European Union was prepared to acknowledge the danger of Iraq's weapons of mass destruction; all that was missing was consensus on what to do about it.

UNMOVIC and Iraqi officials engaged in talks early in May 2002. According to Kofi Annan, secretary-general of the United Nations, this was the first such dialogue since the end of 1998. The renewed hope the talks inspired was short-lived, though, for they ended two months later with no agreement reached. Iraq was looking for assurances that if it complied with UNMOVIC, sanctions would be lifted. Less than a month after the end of these talks, Richard Butler, the former chairman of UNSCOM, told a U.S. Senate committee that Iraq had actually *increased* its production of chemical and biological agents after inspections ended in 1998 and suggested that Iraq was not far from developing nuclear capability. By this time, polls in the United States were showing surprisingly strong American support for war with Iraq—60 percent to 70 percent, even if the action involved ground troops and thus an increased risk of American casualties.

Hearings were held by the Senate Foreign Relations Committee in late July and early August 2002 to explore the consequences of war. So many stories and supposed plans of attack appeared in the media that war began to seem inevitable. The focus of the debate shifted from *whether* to attack Iraq to *how* to attack, especially in light of the continuing U.S. engagement in Afghanistan and the Bush administration's "War on Terror." In an effort to lengthen the path to military engagement, the Senate, and Senator Joseph Biden (Democrat, Delaware) in particular, began to set criteria that President Bush would have to meet in order for Congress to exercise its constitutional power to declare war.

Important issues had to be resolved concerning military action: What was the best way to do it? What would the effects be on the other nations of the world, many of which depended on the United States, Iraq, or both? By mid-August, the administration had put forth no specific plan, and much of the world wondered whether the "regime change" would come to pass. Public support had decreased noticeably but was still around 50 percent. Many suggested that the administration's cause would need the legitimacy that it could get only from institutions such as the U.S. Congress or the United Nations.

By the end of August, after repetitions of the administration's resolve to remove Saddam, countries such as France and Germany began to voice concerns that the United States would move into action before consulting them, and the question of UN-led inspections was raised again.

One of the principal questions in the debate was why

action was necessary at that particular moment. Iraq's military capability was believed to be very low. No evidence of Iraqi mobilization had been found, and no link had been proven between Saddam and Al Qaeda.

By early August 2002, critics were asking why Saddam had to be removed from power at all—why he could not simply be *contained* through continued efforts at disarmament, given that without weapons Saddam's power structure would collapse anyway. Important Republicans began to imply that action against Saddam would not be necessary as long as he remained in his own territory. The political atmosphere was cautious: few politicians wanted to speak publicly against a president with an approval rating as high as that of President Bush, but *no* politicians wanted to rush into ill-justified military action without having explored other options.

U.S. Secretary of Defense Donald Rumsfeld warned on September 19 that the "smoking gun" should not be the goal of inspections: "[T]he last thing we want is a smoking gun. A gun smokes after it's been fired, and the goal must be to stop an attack . . . before it happens." Five days later, British Prime Minister Tony Blair released a dossier that estimated that Saddam would have full nuclear capability in two years if he could find the materials or procure them from someone else or five years if he had to manufacture those materials himself. It was at this point that the phrase *preemptive strike* came into use. Under international law, a preemptive strike is permissible if the acting nation can demonstrate that its opponent is preparing for an attack of its own. If Saddam hated the West and would soon have nuclear capabilities, then could an immediate American attack against him be considered defensive? Debates followed on what a preemptive strike *was* and whether it could be justified. Thus the Bush administration tried to show a link between Saddam and Al Qaeda, the Islamic extremist group that claimed responsibility for the terrorist attack of September 11, 2001; proving this connection would make the

Inspectors from UNMOVIC's inspection team arrive at a presidential palace in Baghdad on December 8, 2002, the day after the Iraqi declaration. The question of UN access to these palaces was as difficult as the question of access to mosques, but Saddam did eventually allow total access. Still, the UN inspectors found Iraqi protest at every site they visited.To come

case for immediate military action.

The administration tried continuously to establish this link. In late September 2002, National Security Advisor Dr. Condoleezza Rice stated explicitly that there were "contacts between senior Iraqi officials and members of [Al Qaeda] going back for actually quite a long time," which were rumored to have been based in chemical weapons, and that Al Qaeda prisoners had claimed that Iraqi officials had trained them in chemical weapons. In November, perhaps acknowledging the general feeling that this link had not been proven, Dr. Rice spoke more generally: "If you look at a regime like Iraq," she said, "with growing capabilities in terms of weapons of mass destruction and with an extreme animus [hostility] towards the United States, and you look at the potential for that to link up with terrorist organizations, including with [Al Qaeda]. You have to be concerned about that." Secretary of State Colin Powell argued this before the UN in February 2003, but the connection remained unclear.

There was the larger issue, too, of the precedent that such a strike would set for other countries at odds—China and Taiwan, for example, or India and Pakistan, both of which have demonstrated some nuclear capability. Should these countries be allowed to strike preemptively? And what of those countries that feel threatened by the United States?

The issue was complicated in mid-October when it was revealed that North Korea had resumed working toward nuclear weapons, in violation of a 1994 treaty with the United States. North Korea had been secretly violating this treaty for eight years while accepting American aid. If preemption was appropriate for Iraq, then why not for North Korea? Striking one of the countries might mean having to strike the other, essentially creating a war with North Korea.

President Bush gave a powerful speech to the UN General Assembly on September 12, "making his case" against Saddam and building support for possible military action. He told skeptical world leaders to confront the "grave and gathering danger" of Iraq or to stand aside as the United States acted alone, and he warned Iraq that military action would be unavoidable if it did not disarm. Deputy Prime Minister Tariq Aziz pointedly called the United States "the administration of evil."

The United States then proposed a new resolution to the UN with strict new rules governing the weapons inspections, loaded with difficult-to-meet conditions in an effort to avoid the interminable delays that might spring up during the inspection process. On September 28, Iraq rejected the wording of this draft completely, and the United States began working on a revision.

Congress was more receptive to President Bush's plans; he persuaded both houses to authorize the use of force against Iraq. Congress did so on October 12, in record time—perhaps in an attempt to rein in the President's actions however possible. (This authorization was called unconstitutional in a lawsuit filed in February 2003, discussed later.) Still, as Election Day 2002 drew near, politicians found public sentiment to be very strongly against war. One Democratic congressman insisted, "There is absolutely no evidence that any thinking person could give that says that we are in any danger from Saddam Hussein today."

Two weeks later, on October 25, the United States and Great Britain submitted a revised draft resolution to the UN. This was only one of several versions then under consideration, France's draft and Russia's being the other major contenders. The principal questions were:

- Should the inspectors have free access to all parts of Iraq, including Saddam's presidential palaces, each of which was really a group of buildings?

- In the event of Iraqi noncompliance, would the United States be authorized to proceed directly to its "preemptive strike," or would it first have to return to the UN for another vote?

- What would the timetable be? (The most likely timetable was 30 days for an initial UNMOVIC report.)

Saddam announced on November 4 that Iraq would be receptive to UN-backed renewal of inspections, provided that the UN resolution did not serve merely as an excuse for U.S.-led military action against Iraq. Four days later, on November 8, the UN at last passed a resolution, Resolution 1441, that would give Iraq one last chance. It established a timetable: Iraq had 7 days to declare cooperation and then 30 days to produce a full and accurate declaration of *all* its programs, including facilities that *could* be used to make weapons. Inspections were to resume within 45 days, with an update to the Security Council within 60 days of that. The resolution appointed UNMOVIC to look for chemical and biological weapons and the International Atomic Energy Agency (IAEA) to look for nuclear facilities. It gave the two agencies unimpeded access to Iraqi facilities and the power to interview Iraqi citizens inside or outside of Iraq. It warned of "serious consequences" for material breaches. The Iraqi parliament deliberated for four days and then rejected the resolution, only to accept it a day later.

On November 18, a preliminary UN inspection team entered Iraq after a four-year hiatus, with inspections scheduled to begin a week later. The team was led by Dr. Hans Blix, a distinguished diplomat educated in Sweden, Britain, and the United States who had served as director of the IAEA.

Because time was such an important factor in any possible military action in Iraq—the Iraqi summer would make maneuvering far more difficult—many observers worried that the length of the process would make military action more difficult. The United States intensified its efforts to create an international coalition *while* the inspections took place. Britain and Canada both joined the cause, and the United States then extended its efforts to include dozens of other countries. Václav Havel, the president of the Czech Republic, urged NATO to consider joining with the United States against Iraq. Germany maintained its position against any use of force. In line with its earlier willingness to accept inspections provided that the United States not be allowed to use noncompliance as a pretext for war, the Iraqi government issued statements accusing the United States of manipulating the UN to further its aggressive goals. Iraqi Foreign Minister Naji Sabri contended to UN Secretary-General Kofi Annan that there were no chemical, biological, or nuclear weapons in Iraq and the United States had not shown otherwise. He further claimed that holding Iraq to a standard of total accuracy in many thousands of pages, produced in haste to meet the UN deadline, was unfair.

Also, it was hard to know what *compliance* would mean once the inspectors actually reached Iraq. Where should they look, and what should they look for? How cooperative would Saddam have to be in order to be deemed compliant? Fears arose that Saddam could use the inspections as a tactic to create delay in military action. The United States would not be able to justify a war if inspectors were still technically doing their job.

The inspectors' first field visit took place on November 27. According to the UN timeline, the inspectors had 60 days, until January 27, to prepare a preliminary report for the UN Security Council. Given that there were 700 or so sites under consideration, the investigation was expected to take a full year, even with full Iraqi compliance. Iraq was expected to produce its "currently accurate, full, and complete declaration" by December 8, 2002.

In the meantime, Saddam tried to restore his damaged relations with Kuwait and Saudi Arabia, largely through free-trade agreements. His public statements portrayed him as a voice of reason and emphasized the militaristic tendencies of the Bush administration, which already had begun to cause alarm in the United States and elsewhere. He also returned some, but not all, of the items Iraq had taken from the Kuwaiti national archive during the 1990 invasion—an issue addressed by the same 1999 UN resolution that created UNMOVIC. Later, on December 7, one of his officials announced a qualified apology for the 1990 invasion of Kuwait. Calling both nations victims of the U.S.-led Gulf War, the speech urged Kuwaitis to join with Iraq against "infidel forces" and even called for the Kuwaitis to expel occupying U.S. troops. The effort was not successful, though, for the speech was denounced by both the Kuwaiti government and the Kuwaiti media.

Saddam's own rhetoric had become relatively conservative but wavered between reassuring and menacing. His administration was saying that he had complied with the inspection program in order to keep his people safe, that the United States was intent on invading Iraq and looking for any excuse to do so, and even that guns had been issued to most Iraqis, who would use them not against the regime, but rather to defend their country against Western aggression. On Wednesday, December 4, the Iraqi vice president, Taha Yassin Ramadan, accused the inspectors of espionage for the United States and Israel and threatened to call in a second team of inspectors, chosen by Iraqi officials from neutral sources, to check every site after UN inspection. Days later, as site after site was visited and revisited and declared "clean," Iraq began a series of challenges to the United States to prove that it possessed banned material of any kind. These challenges continued throughout the inspection process.

The Iraqi disclosure report called for by UN Resolution 1441 was due on December 8, but Iraq handed the report to inspectors a day early. The document was extremely long, consisting of about 12,000 pages, with an 80-page summary and several CDs, and some portions of it were in Arabic. Any analysis of the disclosure would take weeks, and almost immediately it was criticized as a stalling tactic. The Iraqi administration rebutted that the length was due to the Resolution's requirement that all "dual-use" facilities be described in detail. Dual-use facilities included such installations as breweries and factories, and there were many of these in Iraq. The full report made its way to the United Nations headquarters in New York City in two small suitcases. Analysts expected it to declare that Iraq possessed no nuclear, biological, or chemical capabilities, and this was found to be true. The Security Council voted to give full copies of the Iraqi disclosure to its five permanent members—the United States, Great Britain, France, China, and Russia—each of which has the power to veto any resolution. It offered only censored copies (stripped of "biological cookbooks" and "how-to" material on nuclear armaments) to the other ten (non-nuclear) members of the Council. This edited version of the document was approximately 3,000 pages in length.

The components of the declaration that dealt with chemical, biological, and conventional weapons would be analyzed by UNMOVIC, and the nuclear component of the report was given to the IAEA. Only a judgment of compliance would bring about the end of 12 years of sanctions, dating to Iraq's invasion of Kuwait, and the IAEA's director general, Mohamed ElBaradei, said that war could still be avoided if the inspections proved that Saddam had already been effectively disarmed. Now the question became how complete the document was—specifically, whether anything it contained or omitted could be considered grounds for military action under Resolution 1441. War games, involving high-ranking members of the U.S. intelligence program, began in the Qatari desert.

Over the course of the inspections game, Iraq had been asked several times for full disclosure of its weapons programs, and in that decade it had established a history of providing partial reports and then updating them when inspectors found evidence of omissions. An initial report on the 2002 disclosure found that it too was likely to continue this pattern. One of the principal problems was that Iraq had claimed in 1998 to have destroyed hundreds of tons of chemical and biological weapons but had provided no evidence of that destruction. The new disclosure was expected to explain this and thereby answer a question that had troubled observers for four years. Unfortunately, it didn't. The report failed on another important point: It did not explain Iraq's importation or attempted importation of several dual-use items that could be used to manufacture nuclear weapons. In short, it seemed to be only the same material Iraq had submitted over the previous decade, in a new report.

On December 19, U.S. Secretary of State Colin Powell adjudged the declaration as containing flagrant omissions that constituted a "material breach"—and said that Iraq's deceptions could make it impossible to avoid war. Two days later, Dr. Blix urged the United States and the United Kingdom to help out with any intelligence they have concerning Iraq's weapons programs. On January 6, Saddam accused the inspectors of being spies working for the United States. On January 16, inspectors made the minor find of 12 empty chemical warheads. Iraq denied knowledge of these, and Washington referred to them as a "smoldering, not smoking, gun." Two days later, while searching the home of an Iraqi physicist with military connections, the inspection team uncovered 3,000 pages relating to nuclear technology. Hans Blix and Mohamed ElBaradei reported to the Security Council on January 27 and said that, although the inspection team had found no definite evidence of banned activity by the Iraqis, Saddam's regime had not been fully cooperative. The team recommended continuing the inspection program.

The document did not reveal any information significant enough to be brought immediately to the Security Council's attention, so the only thing the Bush administration could do was wait to see whether the inspectors would find a "smoking gun," anything that directly contradicted Iraq's claims, though even if it did find one, other members of the Council could easily call for a second resolution before any action could be taken.

War games continued. The risky smallpox vaccine was administered to 500,000 U.S. troops and to the President himself.

As U.S. bombs moved ever closer to Baghdad, it became ever less clear what exactly it would take to fulfill the "material breach" requirement. According to the UN resolution, the directors of UNMOVIC and the IAEA were obligated to notify the Security Council immediately if they found any violation of the Resolution; presumably, the Council would then discuss and vote on further action. But it was not even clear whose duty it was to decide what was a violation—someone within the Bush administration, such as U.S. Secretary of Defense Donald Rumsfeld, Colin Powell, or President Bush himself? Or Mohamed ElBaradei, or Hans Blix? Or the UN Security Council? Iraq fired on American and British planes in the "no-fly" zones over northern and southern Iraq, but the Security Council had never expressly authorized the air patrols in the first place. Was this a violation? UN Secretary-General Kofi Annan said that it was not, but France, Hans Blix, and Donald Rumsfeld all disagreed.

A greater cause for concern was the mobile laboratories Saddam was believed to have constructed to produce biological weapons. Inspectors might drive all over Iraq without ever pinpointing such a laboratory, and this would make Iraq's noncompliance practically impossible to prove. The game of cat and mouse risked going on forever, and the Bush administration pushed for a decision.

By the end of 2002, most high-profile political figures were vowing to resolve the Iraq problem through diplomacy, but the Middle East was assuming that war would come within months. Saddam continued to claim indignantly that the inspections program would prove him innocent, but defensive training intensified among Iraqi troops and guns were issued to Iraqi citizens. Despite the continued absence of the "smoking gun" that the international community had repeatedly asked the White House to provide, thousands of American and British troops were relocated to the Persian Gulf to prepare for the possibility of invasion. On December 11, President Bush alarmed the world by declaring that any use of weapons of mass destruction against the United States or its allies might result in a nuclear response. Tensions were escalating rapidly.

In mid-December, with the "final" report of the weapons inspectors still more than a month away, the Bush administration pushed UNMOVIC to interview Iraqi scientists who might have been involved in Saddam's weapons program. (UN Resolution 1441 had granted this power to UNMOVIC, even enabling inspectors to remove scientists from the country to ensure their safety.) Hans Blix opposed this step and refused to use the inspections program for "abduction" or as a "defection agency." Even with safe removal from Iraq, though, scientists who volunteered information were clearly in danger. All remembered Hussein Kamal, Saddam's son-in-law and the chief organizer of Iraq's program in weapons of mass destruction, who had defected to Jordan in 1995. He had revealed many Iraqi military secrets and then, having returned to Iraq for his family, had been killed by Saddam.

Also in December, at the urging of the Bush administration, expatriate Iraqi dissidents from multiple groups met first in Iran and then in London to discuss the country's future after Saddam Hussein. There were deep traditional divisions among the groups, but the meeting was important: one of the delegates' primary goals was simply to forestall a potential power vacuum in Iraq, to preserve Iraq's sovereignty in the face of occupation by the West. Although consensus was difficult, and although some favored restoring the Iraqi monarchy, the conference in general seemed to favor installing a democracy.

On December 19, Dr. Blix reported to the UN Security Council that the Iraqi declaration contained nothing that had not been declared in 1998. According to Mohamed ElBaradei, the head of the IAEA, the next step was to verify through inspections and intelligence that the declaration was complete. President Bush declared his hope that war could be avoided. At the close of 2002, military action in Iraq remained a very real possibility, public support was declining, and the Bush administration's rhetoric shifted to "not to conquer, but to *liberate*."

Saddam rallied his own troops on Iraq's Army Day, January 6, which marked the 82nd anniversary of the formation of the Iraqi army. In his speech marking the occasion, he

On February 15, 2003, an estimated 1.5 million people congregated in London's Hyde Park to protest British involvement in the U.S.-led war effort. As the March 17 deadline drew near, British Prime Minister Tony Blair found less and less support among both the British people and the members of Parliament, and there were serious concerns that his siding with the United States might destroy him politically. (The "Make Tea, Not War" poster shows Blair, not U.S. President Bush.) Millions more demonstrated on the same day in major cities around the world.

assured the troops that Iraq would win a conflict with the West because the Iraqi troops were in their homeland and therefore right. He called on Allah to either lead the United States along the road of righteousness or destroy the country completely.

Perhaps with President Bush's "axis of evil" speech in mind, he referred to Americans as "criminals" and as friends and helpers of Satan, night, and darkness. He accused the United States of wanting to divert attention from Israeli crimes against Iraq's "people" in Palestine.

Dr. Blix delivered the inspectors' long-awaited report to the Security Council on January 27, 2003, but he did not say what the United States was hoping he would say. He specified that Iraq had not accounted for 6,500 missing chemical warfare bombs; that it may have turned some nerve gases into weapons and then lied about having done so; that it may have produced more anthrax than it claimed and may still have stockpiles; and that, despite providing access to all sites, it had not shown an understanding of its need to disarm—but he recommended that the inspections be continued. Dr. ElBaradei's report was more optimistic: that although the Iraqis had been only grudgingly cooperative, no evidence of nuclear activity had been found, and with a few more months of work he could declare that Iraq had no nuclear program at all.

The conclusions of the inspectors hardly made the case for war. Rather, they encouraged delay, and it was important to attack before the end of February, when the Iraqi spring would bring flooding, heavy rains, and oppressive heat. In his annual State of the Union Address on the following day, President Bush announced that U.S. Secretary of State Colin Powell would address the Security Council to "present information and intelligence about Iraq's illegal weapons programs, its attempt to hide those weapons from inspectors, and its links to terrorist groups." He reaffirmed his resolve to see Saddam neutralized: "We will consult. But let there be no misunderstanding: If Saddam Hussein does not fully disarm, for the safety of our people and for the peace of the world, we will lead a coalition to disarm him." Moreover, he expressed sympathy for the Iraqi people: "[T]onight I have a message for the brave and oppressed people of Iraq: Your enemy is not surrounding your country; your enemy is *ruling* your country. And the day he and his regime are removed from power will be the day of your liberation."

By this time, Saddam was calling on the UN "to shoulder its responsibilities to protect Iraq from this colonial administration which is blinded by its oil fever" and warning that a U.S.-led invasion of Iraq would be like the endless and costly Vietnam War. Several nations raised the hope that he would simply abdicate and exile himself, and Saudi Arabia met with him to discuss the prospect. The U.S. government even offered to find him a new country in which to live.

President Bush chose Colin Powell to address the UN Security Council because Powell was the only member of the administration whom the anti-war world considered an ally. On February 5, 2003, Powell argued before the UN that the issue with Iraq was not *cooperation* but *disarmament*—and that the validity of the UN itself was at stake. He accused Iraq of conducting deadly chemical experiments on 1,600 people. He restated the tenuous case for a link between Saddam and Al Qaeda, and he played audiotapes that seemed to threaten Mohamed ElBaradei with nerve agents and that suggested that Iraq was blocking inspections and hiding weapons. He claimed that Iraqi scientists had been threatened with execution if they agreed to be interviewed outside Iraq. He showed satellite images of military facilities active at the beginning of the inspections, and he estimated that Iraq had 2 of 3 components necessary for nuclear weapons and 100 to 500 tons of chemical agents. He called Iraq's material breach of Resolution 1441 "irrefutable and undeniable."

Even France and Germany found the evidence compelling, though they still were not convinced that war was necessary. France moved to strengthen the inspections but to give UNMOVIC and the IAEA more time. The first Iraqi scientist to be interviewed without a government "minder" was interviewed on the following day. On February 7, Saddam gave inspectors access to two top-secret sites that Powell had mentioned as points of contention.

The combined pressure of the UN forces, the military buildup in the region, and the international community seemed to be having an effect on the Iraqi regime. On February 9, after two days of talks with Dr. Blix, Iraq offered more information on its chemical and biological programs and spoke of banning nuclear, chemical, and biological weapons by law within its borders. It became likely that Saddam would allow U-2 spy planes to enter Iraqi air space, and on February 10 he did. Nevertheless, the U.S. ambassador to the UN, John Negroponte, began to push for a resolution that authorized war—and he used the word "days."

Meanwhile, thousands thronged the streets of major Iraqi cities, many with automatic weapons and portraits of Saddam. The Iraqi government reveled in the worldwide anti-war protests spurred by Powell's speech, Saddam's appearance of cooperation, and the intense military buildup in the region. The Iraqi media, heavily controlled by the government, spoke out against American "aggression."

Despite continued talk of peaceful resolution, military buildup continued. Some 200,000 troops had been deployed to the region by the end of February, as well as several battleships and other key equipment, and hundreds of war planners had been moved from Florida to friendly Qatar. Saddam, too, prepared: he arranged the Republican Guard in rings around Baghdad and fortified the city with troops, missile batteries, and mounds of earth.

On February 19, U.S. Secretary of Defense Donald Rumsfeld declared that there were three eventualities that could prevent war: Saddam's compliance with UN resolutions, Saddam's exile, and an overthrow of Saddam's regime from within Iraq. All of these were possible, and each was becoming more likely as masses of soldiers gathered in allied countries— but whether enough could be done in time was unclear.

By March 2003, almost 300,000 troops were massed at Iraqi borders. Preparations were not quite complete, but all forces declared readiness to attack. On March 17, despite a failed attempt at a UN resolutionauthorizing war, President Bush gave Saddam 48 hours to leave Iraq in order to avoid "military conflict." The Saudis had tried to persuade Saddam to abdicate, but it was unlikely that he would give up power without a fight.

9

The Strongman at War

The Iraqis don't wish war, but if war is imposed upon them, if they are attacked and insulted, they will defend themselves. They will defend their country, their sovereignty, and their security. We will not disappoint those who believe in the principles of justice, and we will uphold the principles of justice and right that we strongly believe in.

—SADDAM HUSSEIN
TO FORMER BRITISH LABOUR CABINET MINISTER TONY BENN,
FEBRUARY 4, 2003

In mid-February 2003, inspectors found ten Al Samoud 2 missiles filled with mustard gas that had a range greater than the 93 miles (150 km) allowed by UN sanctions. These had been found before, by the inspectors who left in 1998, but Iraq did not declare them in the December 7 document. Iraq argued that the testing methods had been faulty and that the missiles could not reach any other country, and it refused to destroy them. Dr. Blix later ordered UNMOVIC to do so. Critics took this incident as an important sign that Iraq was hiding munitions—and wondered what other weapons Saddam had not declared.

Even if the United States went to war with Iraq without the UN's support, American chances would be good. Excluding its potential chemical and biological stocks, estimates of Iraq's active military strength include 424,000 active troops; 1,900 tanks; 2,400 armored personnel carriers; 1,900 wheeled guns; 300 combat aircraft; and some short-range rocket systems. By all accounts, though, Iraq has not been able to modernize its armed forces or to obtain the spare parts necessary to keep all its equipment in service. Ten years after the invasion of Kuwait, Iraq's armed forces are not much of a match for the military strength and the intelligence-gathering and targeting technology that the United States has developed since the first Gulf War. Of course, Iraq probably does have some chemical and biological stocks left that it has hidden from inspectors or that inspectors simply have not yet destroyed. Or it may have given some of these to other anti-U.S. groups, such as Al Qaeda operatives in the north, for safekeeping. Iraq's true military strength is hard to gauge.

At least 200,000 troops would be needed for an invasion, most of which were already positioned by February 2003, as well as hundreds of aircraft, ships, and support vehicles. But would taking on Iraq tax the American military too much? Documents surfaced in 2002 and 2003 that suggested that Osama bin Laden was still alive and Al Qaeda still active, raising the question of whether the War on Terror would have to be run concurrently with a war in Iraq. The military complex raised this point when military action in Iraq was first discussed; it would be difficult to face the country's obligations in Afghanistan (and any more sites in the War on Terror), Iraq, and the security concerns within the United States all at the same time. Adding possible conflict in North Korea to the mix makes the future of

American military resources even more uncertain.

Also, the costs of a war with Iraq would be high. The military action in Afghanistan used mostly air forces and Special Forces and so was relatively inexpensive, but the possibility of doing this again in Iraq was slim. Estimates of the cost of war with Iraq ranged in September 2002 from a very conservative $50 billion to $200 billion, and by 2003 they jumped to $300 or $400 billion.

"Going it alone" would divide the attention of the American military at a crucial time and would drain federal budgets. Although the Bush administration has distanced itself politically from the UN, it was believed that war in Iraq would be most effective with the support of other countries and of groups within Iraq.

The issue split Europe. Great Britain has been an ally of the United States since the beginning, even over British anti-war protest massive enough to jeopardize Prime Minister Tony Blair's political position. Australia and Canada initially showed support. On January 30, 2003, eight nations—the Czech Republic, Italy, Denmark, Spain, Portugal, Poland, Hungary, and Great Britain—signed a letter of support for an invasion of Iraq. France and Germany did not sign the letter; together they took Europe's most aggressive stance against war. Germany fears destabilization of the region and has spoken against military action from the start. France has always favored extending the inspection program; it proposed in 2002 that a second Security Council resolution be required before war could be declared. France was dogged in its opposition and even threatened to deny membership in the European Union (EU) to three applicant countries—Poland, Hungary, and the Czech Republic—that signed the letter of support in January. Both France and Germany have an economic interest in postwar Iraq, though, so it seemed likely that they would participate in some way if an invasion took place.

The division among the European countries, which have

tried to unite as the European Union, became so alarming that in mid-February 2003 the EU's 15 member nations met at an emergency summit in Brussels to determine the EU's official position. Great Britain acknowledged the public sentiment against war—five million people had protested around the world on one weekend—and agreed to allow more time for inspections, as long as there was a definite ending point. France argued that only the inspectors should be able to determine that "point of no return." Germany was willing to go along with the EU consensus that war remained a possibility but maintained that the focus should be on resolving the conflict peacefully. The summit ended with a decision to give Iraq an unspecified amount of time, to acknowledge that war might be necessary, and to encourage the resumption of peace talks between Israel and Palestine—a fundamental Middle Eastern conflict that results in much anti-Western sentiment throughout the region. The EU's draft declaration declared that time was "rapidly running out" for Saddam to comply, but on Germany's insistence this phrase was taken out.

Russia, one of the five veto-wielding members of the UN Security Council, was initially noncommittal, then spoke out for extending inspections. Its position is complicated by the fact that it has commercial ties with Iran, Iraq, *and* North Korea—all three members of the Bush administration's "axis of evil." Moreover, Iraq owes Russia approximately $8 billion, so Russia has an interest in Iraq's economic stability. But President Bush had guaranteed that the United States would protect Russia's interest after the war, and this guarantee seemed to make Russia far more likely to become an ally.

Asia was less likely in general to become involved. China is one of the five permanent members of the UN Security Council and thus has the power to veto any proposed resolution. Like France, Germany, and most other nations, it supported the inspection program and preferred not to rush into open conflict. It may be more concerned with the emerging issue of

The Iraqi forces were using outdated and ill-maintained equipment, but they nevertheless outnumbered coalition troops. The loyalty of the Iraqi military was hard to gauge. Members repeatedly declared allegiance to Saddam, but it was possible that their loyalties would shift in the heat of battle. The support of the Iraqi military would mean a much faster and cleaner war.

North Korea, though, and its position was unclear. Japan's constitution prohibits it from actively giving military aid, and although it made a small exception in Afghanistan, it is unlikely to continue that pattern.

While European and Asian support was important politically, Middle Eastern support was necessary to carry out the war. Air strikes against Iraq require the use of airbases in neighboring countries, such as Kuwait, Qatar, Saudi Arabia, and Turkey.

Among the Arab and Middle Eastern nations, though, the situation is extremely complex. The alliance of Arab, Western, and other states that fought Iraq during the Persian Gulf War fell apart in the 1990s. Continual warnings about the threat that Iraq posed to the region wore thin among Arabs as American and British bombs destroyed the Iraqi capital, and angry street demonstrations have prompted governments to oppose any more remote-control bombings. Egypt's president, Hosni Mubarak, has demanded an end to air strikes. Some Arab newspapers began to call for retaliation against the United States and Great Britain. Even Morocco, which usually is friendly toward the United States, saw a demonstration of thousands of students in its capital, Rabat.

At the root of much of the conflict is the close relationship between the United States and Israel, a nation that much of the Middle East despises. (Israel has been attacked by Saddam before and pressed for immediate military action, even though if defeated Saddam may turn his weapons against Israel once again.) Still, the United States does have supporters in the region. Kuwait, Qatar, and Bahrain are the strongest of these, and all have provided military support in some form, even though all preferred a diplomatic solution. Kuwait and Qatar both have housed coalition troops and provided sites for combat training. Oman and the United Arab Emirates also have sent troops and equipment to Kuwait, which shares a border with Iraq and which Iraq invaded in the Gulf War. Most other nations in the region are deeply conflicted—disliking Saddam, afraid of the consequences of war, favoring Arabs over Westerners, navigating complicated commercial and political relationships, and trying to postpone committing to any side.

Among the most important Middle Eastern nations to gain as allies in war with Iraq are those that actually share a border with Iraq: Saudi Arabia, Jordan, Syria, Turkey, and Iran.

Saudi Arabia is considered the United States' greatest ally in the Middle East, and any invasion of Iraq depended on Saudi support. Saudi Arabia's relationship with the United States has been good for many years, largely because of the booming oil trade and Saudi investments in American corporations. But Saudi popularity in the United States plummeted when Americans learned that many of the September 11 hijackers had Saudi connections, and it was further damaged when funds from Saudi sources were revealed to have supported Al Qaeda. The relationship between the countries also depends, once again, on U.S. policy toward Israel. The Saudis have told Washington clearly that the future of Iraq is not as important to the Arab world as the future of Palestine, and if the United States supports Israel too openly then the Saudi relationship may dissolve, barring American use of crucial Saudi bases, resources, and even air space. The relationship is now strained, and Saudi Arabia has vacillated between allowing the United States to use its bases and refusing this permission.

Jordan is officially against military action, and many popular demonstrations there have shown this feeling to be strong among the Jordanian people. Iraq, Russia, and Syria are among Jordan's most important partners in trade, and Jordan depends on Iraq for *all* its oil. Jordan has repeatedly called for an end to economic sanctions against Iraq, and in 1991 there were even pro-Saddam demonstrations. Like many Iraqis and others in the Middle East, many Jordanians believe that the United States has created a crisis in Iraq in order to tighten its grip on the region and to ensure its own access to Iraqi oil. Also, much of the Jordanian population is of Palestinian origin, no friend to Israel, so Jordan argues that the more important conflict is the one between Israel and Palestine. Still, Jordan's relationship with the United States is vital to its survival.Syria, Iraq, Iran, Armenia, and Turkey share a political problem that indirectly affects most other countries in the region as well: the Kurdish desire for a homeland. The Kurds have been nomadic herders for millennia, and in that time many rulers of the region have tried to extinguish their cultural identity. They lived in military alliance with the Ottoman Empire (now Turkey) for centuries until the Empire claimed their land; a century of revolts followed. The Kurds were to be given their own land—the country of Kurdistan—after the Empire fell in World War I, but this never happened. Since that time, they have lived in a loosely defined territory that spans several countries. Today, 15 to 20 million live in Turkey, 10 million in Iran, 1.5 million in Syria, 500,000 in the former Soviet Union, and 4 million in Iraq.

With Iranian support, the Iraqi Kurds posed enough of a threat to the Ba'ath regime in its early years to be granted self-rule wherever they formed a majority of the population. The borders of this region of northern Iraq, the Kurdish Autonomous Region, were decided in 1974. Most Kurds are Sunni Muslim, like much of the Ba'ath party, but they sided with Shi'ite Iran again during the Iran–Iraq War (1980–1988), and they have suffered from Saddam's retaliations ever since. Great Britain and the United States established the northern "no-fly" zone in 1991 as a means of protecting the Kurds, and this has enabled the Iraqi Kurds to find some prosperity. Still, the Kurdish groups are scattered and divided. They are considered the world's largest stateless population, and Kurdish revolts erupt repeatedly throughout the region informally known as Kurdistan. Iran, Iraq, Turkey, Syria, and the other nations with Kurdish populations try to keep Kurdish nationalism in check.

Syria and Iran are both very sensitive to the Kurdish question. More generally, both might like to see Saddam removed from power, but both fear that military intervention would result in a "puppet regime" that would increase the influence of the West. Syria helped the U.S.-led coalition in the Gulf War but now worries more about an alliance between Israel and Turkey than about Iraq; in fact, surprisingly, Syria has become known as Iraq's "best friend" on the Security Council. (Two nations abstained from the vote restricting Saddam's purchasing power through the oil-for-food program: Russia and Syria.)

Turkey initially agreed to support any military action authorized by the United Nations. It was one of the few nations willing to provide military bases at first, and it has allowed its territory as a base for American and British patrols of the "no-fly" zone. Continued use of Turkish bases would have enabled a coalition to wage war against Iraq on multiple fronts—a significant tactical advantage. But Turkey has serious concerns about the consequences of war. Turkey does not officially recognize the Kurds as a minority population, but it shares borders with both Iraq and Kurdistan and, like Syria and Iran, has a Kurdish population in the millions. Many Turkish Kurds are refugees from Saddam's attacks. All nations worry that any alliance between the Iraqi Kurds and a victorious Western coalition will induce their own Kurdish populations to push for independence—and Turkey has already been fighting separatist revolts for decades.

But there are also less political concerns. The Turkish population is relatively pro-West, but also mostly Muslim, and Turkey's participation in military exercises with the United States and Israel has isolated it from the rest of the Muslim community. Opinion polls have shown that 90 percent oppose war with another Muslim country. Turkey was unlikely to deploy troops, in any case, and it signed an agreement with Egypt to prevent a U.S.-led war.

Turkey is also in a vulnerable geographic position. Aside from any danger from Saddam, the Kurds in northern Iraq may try to capture oil-rich cities in northern Turkey. Even NATO recognizes the danger: early in 2003, NATO resolved to send surveillance aircraft, Patriot missiles, and biochemical defense systems to Turkey, its only member that borders Iraq. (The attempt was blocked at first by France, Germany, and Belgium, who saw the preparations as condoning war, but it ultimately succeeded.) Because of its precarious position and reluctance to fight, Turkey's initial commitment has wavered, and its government has demanded written guarantees of its role in war and reconstruction and of all economic aid it would receive in return for the use of its bases. The United States offered billions of dollars for assistance and loans to Turkey but in the end was refused the use of Turkey as a base to launch both land and air forces.

Regardless of the strength of an international coalition, though, local support would be crucial, especially in the power vacuum that would follow a toppled regime. The United States does have supporters in Iraq, but most of them are wary. Some are afraid to speak out against Saddam, who won 100 percent of the vote in the election of October 15, 2002. Some refuse to be used merely as ground troops by Western forces. Some have been disappointed by the United States in uprisings before and hesitate to trust the United States again. The splinter groups in Iraq—religious, political, and military—have been cowed by Saddam's brutality. Opposition groups in exile are mostly badly run and have little popular support in Iraq. No strong unifying leadership might come from those opposition groups if Saddam were removed from power.

The responses of the Iraqi citizenry are hard to gauge. Some supported the inspection program as a way of proving to the world that Iraq had nothing to hide. Many considered the inspections invasive—particularly those of personal effects and the presidential palaces. Some even found them destructive, and a few angrily vowed to seek compensation from the UN for damage to their property. Some believed that the inspections were really a way for the Bush administration to carry out pre-war reconnaissance. Of particular concern to the Iraqis were the inspections of mosques, which many of Iraqi's faithful saw as an insult to Islam. But Saddam has built many mosques over the past decade, and the inspectors needed to satisfy the UN that he has done this out of purely religious motives. Iraqi officials declared themselves eager to cooperate in order to avoid giving the Bush administration a pretext for war. There was

Saddam (left) is seen here with his son Qusay, who is presumed to be his heir to power. Qusay oversees all Iraqi intelligence and the Republican Guard and is known for using "tools of repression"— including interrogation, detainment, blackmail, and violence—to eliminate his father's political opposition. Qusay was elected to the Iraqi Regional Command, which runs the Ba'ath party, in 2001.

also the possibility that cooperation would lead to a lifting of the sanctions that have crippled Iraq since the first Gulf War.

One of Saddam's most valued allies throughout the process has been the state-controlled Iraqi media, which Saddam encouraged to film every empty-handed weapons inspector possible.

There are more than 70 opposition groups operating inside and outside of Iraq. President Bush has designated six of these as democratic opposition and thus potential allies in his push for "regime change": the Iraqi National Accord, the Iraqi

National Congress, the Constitutional Monarchy Movement, the Supreme Council for Islamic Revolution in Iraq, the Kurdish Democratic Party, and the Patriotic Union of Kurdistan.

The Iraqi National Accord (INA) is composed mainly of insiders from Iraq's national security and intelligence programs, some of whom still live in Iraq. Jordan, Kuwait, Saudi Arabia, and the U.S. government have supported its commitment to democracy. It was further strengthened by the defection of Hussein Kamal in 1995, but a year later Saddam became aware of its operations and executed dozens of its members.

The Iraqi National Congress (INC) has been trying to overthrow Saddam since 1992 and made an unsuccessful attempt in 1995. It has been one of the most popular opposition groups and received most of the $96 million in aid given by President Clinton in 1998. It leader, Ahmad Chalabi, is backed by much of the U.S. government but has a dubious past and has been criticized as an opportunist. It is uncertain whether the INC would be an effective ally in postwar Iraq. The Constitutional Monarchy Movement (CMM) is led by Sharif Ali bin al-Hussein, the heir apparent to the Hashemite dynasty, who defends a constitutional monarchy within a parliamentary system of democracy.

The Supreme Council for Islamic Revolution in Iraq (SCIRI), composed mainly of Shi'ite exiles, is supported by most of Iraq's Shi'ite population (60–65 percent of the total) and by Iran. It is based in Tehran, where its leader resides. SCIRI controls between 7,000 and 15,000 guerrilla troops in Iraq and about 3,000 troops in Iran near the Iraqi border. The Shi'ite Muslims rose against Saddam in 1991 and 1999, with U.S. backing, but failed, so it is uncertain whether SCIRI or Iran would side with the United States again. The United States has criticized SCIRI's political tactics in the past, and would prefer a regime not led by Shi'ites with close ties to Iran.

The Kurdistan Democratic Party (KDP) and the Patriotic Union of Kurdistan (PUK) represent the Kurds in the north.

Saddam has used chemical weapons on the Kurds in the past, and they would be glad to see him out of power, especially because they might gain the autonomy they desire. Still, the Kurds have economic ties to Saddam, and they profit immensely from smuggling oil, which would not be possible without the UN sanctions against the current regime. The two parties were one and the same before 1975, and they have tried to work together again. Americans are relatively welcome in the Kurdish Autonomous Region, but the Kurds are also wary of being controlled by the West. Rumors that the United States might ask or permit Turkey to send 80,000 troops into Iraq threatened to damage the relationship seriously.

Continuing a trend begun by President Clinton in 1998, President Bush ordered the Department of Defense to provide about $92 million in aid to these factions. All six were invited to Washington in August 2002 for the first of several conferences on post-Saddam Iraq. Unfortunately, the United States has encouraged revolt among Iraqi dissidents several times in the past but has always failed to support them. For example, in 1991 Iraqis in the north and south rebelled, partly in response to U.S. urging; thousands were killed when the United States backed out and the uprisings were crushed by the Iraqi army. In 1995 and 1996, Saddam put down CIA-sponsored rebellions in northern Iraq when U.S. air cover failed to materialize. After these experiences, Iraqi factions that might oppose Saddam are unlikely to respond quickly to another American call to arms, and the politics of dealing with them might be too complex.

A better choice for local support, then, may be the Iraqi army, with or without the direct assistance of the Iraqi National Accord. The very existence of the INA suggests that there are even more officers in the current Iraqi military who would support a new regime—though of course some of the officers have a stake in the survival of Saddam's regime. The army's preparedness and relative stability would make it a valuable ally. The army might be the only institution that could overthrow

Saddam and control the country, but Iraq has been down a similar road several times before in the 20th century, with mixed results. In any case, reports say senior army posts are rotated regularly, army units stationed near Baghdad have no ammunition in their guns, and only a tiny number of people know about the president's whereabouts and movements. Senior army officers, who by Iraqi standards lead privileged lives, have repaid the president with loyalty. Many of them might refuse to back a new government if Saddam Hussein fell.

If war is successful, then what will happen after Saddam is deposed? He has been in power since 1979, with Washington trying to oust him since 1990, and in that time he has done little to establish a line of political succession. His two sons, Uday and Qusay, seem the only likely candidates to succeed him if his regime survives.

Because Saddam's rule has been so absolute, removing him would leave a serious power vacuum—-so serious that most Middle Eastern governments would rather see Saddam stay in power than face the prospect of civil war and the disintegration of the country. Iraq might break into three its three components: the Kurds in the north, the Shi'ite Muslims in the south, and the Sunni Muslims in the center. The creation of a Shi'ite state would be a victory for fundamentalist-Islamic Iran; but even if that were to happen, Iran and Syria would fear the rise of Kurdish nationalist and separatist movements. The Kurds are the largest group in the world with no official homeland, and their situation in Iraq's Kurdish Autonomous Region is volatile. Much of the Middle East worries about the effects of breaking Saddam's hold on the Kurds.

Although many accuse the United States of "oil fever" and waging war to advance economic interest, American need for Iraqi oil is not as great as many think. Saddam is limiting the current Iraqi supply, and the United States does have other resources, including its own production. More important is the question of diffusion—what would happen if other countries, because of sabotage or for any other reason, decreased the flow of oil from *their* wells? Especially in light of the political crisis that destabilized Venezuela, another major supplier, in 2002, the negative impact on the American economy could be considerable. But even putting aside the issue of Iraqi oil, no one could fail to see the strategic position that Iraq holds in the Middle East and the advantage of having a presence there.

At Fort Hood, in his home state of Texas, on January 3, 2003, President Bush spoke again of the possibility of resolving the conflict peacefully, all the while building up morale in the military: "We prefer voluntary compliance from Iraq. Force is our last choice, but if force becomes necessary to disarm Iraq of weapons of mass destruction . . . to secure our country and to keep the peace, America will act deliberately, America will act decisively, and America will prevail because we've got the finest military in the world."

As the days went by, it became clear that a peaceful resolution would not come to pass. In one of his briefings with them, Dr. Blix of UNMOVIC told the UN Security Council that, although it was grudgingly cooperating, Iraq did not seem to feel the need to disarm. The Administration's attempts to fashion a second resolution to present at the UN that would bring others into its "coalition of the willing" were faced down by a sure veto by France. On Sunday, March 16, 2003, the United States, the United Kingdom, Spain, and Portugal met in the Azores Islands, in the middle of the Atlantic Ocean, to discuss what, if any, diplomatic options were still open to them. On Monday, March 17, President Bush issued a call to Saddam Hussein to leave Iraq within 48 hours or face war. Iraq quickly rejected the ultimatum saying that Hussein and his family would never leave Iraq. On the evening of March 19, the United States and Great Britain launched a war against Iraq after President Bush's deadline to Hussein passed unheeded. In Baghdad, during the pre-dawn hours of March 20, the second Persian Gulf War began.

1937 **April 28** Saddam Hussein born in the village of Ouja, near Tikrit in northern Iraq.

1957 Joins the Ba'ath party at the age of 19.

1959 Participates in assassination attempt against Abdul Karim Qasim, Prime Minister of Iraq after the 1958 revolution. Flees to Egypt, where he spends the next four years.

1963 **February–November** Takes charge of organizing a Ba'ath security organ, "Jihaz Haneen,"the core of the Iraqi security force after 1968.

1964 **September 4** Saddam imprisoned for failed coup attempt.

1968 **July 17–30** Bloodless coup by senior Arab Nationalist officers and retired Ba'athist officers. Ahmed Hassan al-Bakr, a relative of Saddam, becomes president and chairman of the Revolutionary Command Council (RCC).

July 30 Saddam carries out a plot to oust the rival faction (Arab Nationalist officers) in the coup.

Fall Beginning of purges to remove all non-Ba'athists from posts within state institutions. Members of non-Ba'ath political parties and non-Arabs are accused of crimes and executed or deported.

1975 **March 6** Saddam signs Algiers Accord with the Shah of Iran. The Accord defines border with Iran and ends Iranian support for Kurds.

March–April Major exodus of Kurds to Iran.

1979 **July 16** President al-Bakr retires and Saddam Hussein, 42, is sworn in as President of the Republic of Iraq.

1980 **September** Saddam publicly tears up the 1975 Algiers Accord. Iraqi Air Force bombs Iranian airfields and Iraqi forces invade Iran.

1988 **March** The Kurdish town of Halabja is gassed, killing 5,000.

August Cease-fire declared between Iraq and Iran, ending the 8-year war. War is estimated to have caused one million casualties, including 250,000 Iraqi dead.

1990 **August 2** Iraqi troops cross into Kuwait and occupy the country, ejecting the Kuwaiti government.

August 28 Kuwait officially becomes the 19th province of Iraq. Arab League defects to American coalition, sending troops to help U.S. defend Saudi Arabia from Iraq.

1991   **January 17** Allied planes begin bombing Iraq. U.S.-led international alliance drives Saddam Hussein's army out of Kuwait.

1995   Two daughters and sons-in-law defect to Jordan but later return to Iraq on promises of forgiveness. Saddam has the men killed; his wife protests bitterly and is placed under house arrest.

1996   The Washington Post reveals a plot against Saddam financed by the CIA that cost $100 million but did not achieve its goal: to help Iraqi resisters in the overthrow of the Saddam regime.

December Uday Hussein, 32, Saddam's eldest son and heir apparent, is gravely wounded by two gunmen close to Iraqi intelligence headquarters. A purge follows; hundreds are executed and thousands arrested, but identity of gunmen remains unknown.

1998   **October 31** Iraq ends all forms of cooperation with the United Nations (UN) Special Commission on Iraq (Unscom).

December 16–19 After UN staff are evacuated from Baghdad, the United States and Great Britain launch a bombing campaign, "Operation Desert Fox," to destroy Iraq's nuclear, chemical, and biological weapons programs.

2000   **August** Baghdad airport reopens, followed by a stream of international flights organized by countries and organizations campaigning against sanctions.

November Deputy Prime Minister Tariq Aziz rejects new weapons inspection proposals.

2001   **February** Britain and the United States carry out bombing raids to try to disable Iraq's air defense network. The bombings have little international support. Iraq complains about ongoing raids.

May Saddam Hussein's son Qusay elected to the leadership of the ruling Ba'ath Party, fueling speculation that he's being groomed to succeed his father.

2002   **January** Iraq invites a UN human rights expert to visit for the first time since envoys were banned from the country in 1992.

April Deputy Prime Minister Tariq Aziz announces that Iraq is prepared to allowed UN weapons inspectors back into the country.

May Iraqi officials engage in talks with UNMOVIC; these end unsuccessfully two months later.

2002 **August** Discussion of "regime change" has begun in the United States.

September 12 U.S. President Bush warns the UN General Assembly to confront the "grave and gathering danger" of Iraq.

October 12 The U.S. Congress authorizes President Bush to use force against Iraq.

October 25 The United States and Britain propose the resolution that will become Resolution 1441.

November 8 The UN passes Resolution 1441, setting deadlines for inspections and Iraqi cooperation.

November 18 Inspectors return to Iraq.

December 7 Iraqi officials submit their 12,000-page weapons declaration to UNMOVIC inspectors a day early. U.S. Secretary of State Colin Powell says that the document's omissions constitute a "material breach,"; on December 19, Dr. Blix announces that the document contains no new information.

December Expatriate Iraqi groups meet in London and elsewhere to discuss the post-Saddam future.

2003 **January 27** Hans Blix and Mohamed ElBaradei report to the Security Council that they have found nothing but that Iraqi cooperation has been limited.

February 5 Colin Powell argues before the Security Council that disarmament is necessary to preserve the validity of the UN.

February 10 After offering more information on its weapons programs and announcing intentions to ban banned weapons, Iraq allows U-2 spy planes to enter its airspace.

February 15 Anti-war protests break out around the world.

March 17 After an unsuccessful attempt to secure a UN resolution authorizing war, President Bush delivers the 48-hour ultimatum.

March 19 At 9:34 P.M. (EST), the second Persian Gulf War begins.

Aburish, Saïd K. *Saddam Hussein: The Politics of Revenge.* New York: Bloomsbury, 2000.

al-Khalil, Samir. *Republic of Fear: The Inside Story of Saddam's Iraq.* New York: Pantheon Books, 1990.

Baram, Mamatzia. *Building Toward Crisis: Saddam Husayn's Strategy For Survival.* Washington, DC: Washington Institute for Near East Policy, 1998.

Bhatia, Shyam and Daniel McGrory. *Brighter Than the Baghdad Sun: Saddam Hussein's Nuclear Threat to the United States.* Washington, DC: Regnery Publications, 2000.

Bowden, Mark. "Tales of the Tyrant: The Private Life and Inner World of Saddam Hussein." *The Atlantic Monthly.* May, 2002.

Cipkowski, Peter. *Understanding the Crisis in the Persian Gulf.* New York: John Wiley & Sons, Inc., 1992.

Cockburn, Andrew and Patrick Cockburn. *Out of the Ashes: The Resurrection of Saddam Hussein.* New York: HarperCollins Publishers, 1999.

Darwish, Adel and Gregory Alexander. *Unholy Babylon: The Secret History of Saddam's War.* New York: St. Martin's Press, 1991.

Deegan, Paul J. *Saddam Hussein.* Edina, Minn.: Abdo & Daughters, 1991.

Gordon, Michael R. "Radio Transmitter to Oppose Hussein Wins US Backing." *The New York Times.* February 28, 2002.

Hamza, Khidhir with Jeff Stein. *Saddam's Bombmaker: The Terrifying Story of the Iraqi Nuclear and Biological Weapons Agenda.* New York: Scribner, 2000.

Henderson, Simon. *Instant Empire: Saddam Hussein's Ambition for Iraq.* San Francisco: Mercury House, 1991.

Miller, Judith and Laurie Mylroie. *Saddam Hussein and the Crisis in the Gulf.* New York: Times Books/Random House, 1990.

Myerson, Daniel. *Blood and Splendor: The Lives of Five Tyrants, from Nero to Saddam Hussein.* New York: Perennial, 2000.

Renfrew, Nita M. *Saddam Hussein.* New York: Chelsea House, 1992.

Stefoff, Rebecca. *Saddam Hussein.* Brookfield, Conn.: Millbrook Press, 1995.

WEB SITES

United Nations Security Council: Iraq Crisis
www.globalpolicy.org/security/issues/irqindx.htm

U.S. Central Intelligence Agency: The World Factbook: Iraq
www.cia.gov/cia/publications/factbook/geos/iz.html

The Iraq Information Network
www.iraq.net/

The Iraq Foundation
www.iraqfoundation.org/

U.S. Library of Congress: Iraq: A Country Study
memory.loc.gov/frd/cs/iqtoc.html

Radio Free Iraq
www.rferl.org/bd/iq/

U.S. Department of State: Iraq
www.state.gov/p/nea/ci/c3212.htm

CHARLES J. SHIELDS is the author of 35 books for young people, primarily histories and biographies. His 1988 book *The College Guide for Parents* (The College Board), won a Distinguished Achievement Award from the Educational Press Association. In 1995, he was recognized by the State of Illinois as one of "Those Who Excel in Education." Until 1997, he was chairman of the English department at Homewood-Flossmoor High School in Flossmoor, Illinois. Since then, he has been writing full-time.

ARTHUR M. SCHLESINGER, jr. is the leading American historian of our time. He won the Pulitzer Prize for his book *The Age of Jackson* (1945) and again for a chronicle of the Kennedy Administration, *A Thousand Days* (1965), which also won the National Book Award. Professor Schlesinger is the Albert Schweitzer Professor of the Humanities at the City University of New York and has been involved in several other Chelsea House projects, including the series REVOLUTIONARY WAR LEADERS, COLONIAL LEADERS, and YOUR GOVERNMENT.